BEHIND *the* FAÇADE

The dining room, Manderston House, Berwickshire. The original house was remodelled by John Kinross 1903–5, to reflect the wealth and status of its new owner, and transform it into one of the most opulent of Scottish Edwardian country houses.

BEHIND *the* FAÇADE

Four centuries of Scottish Interiors

Sheila Mackay

Foreword by John Gifford

RCAHMS

EDINBURGH : HMSO

© Text: Sheila Mackay 1995
© Illustrations RCAHMS unless otherwise stated
First published 1995

Designed by Graham Galloway FCSD
HMSO Graphic Design
Edited by Stephanie Pickering

British Library Cataloguing in Publication Data
A catalogue record for this book is available from the British Library

ISBN 0 11 495239 6

RCAHMS
NMRS

ROYAL COMMISSION ON THE ANCIENT AND HISTORICAL MONUMENTS OF SCOTLAND
John Sinclair House, 16 Bernard Terrace, Edinburgh EH8 9NX

Applications for copies of illustrations and permission to reproduce should be made to the Secretary.

The Royal Commission, founded in 1908, is the national body of survey and record for archaeological sites and historic buildings of all types and periods. The record is made available and interpreted through the central public archive, the National Monuments Record of Scotland at the address above, and through a wide range of topographical and thematic publications.

The illustrations in this book are from the National Monuments Record of the Royal Commission on the Ancient and Historical Monuments of Scotland with the following exceptions which are identified by page number and position: *8, 34R, 35, 40R, 174* National Galleries of Scotland; *33, 34, 42* Historic Scotland; *36* and *40* Flora Maxwell Stuart /Jarrold Publishing; *45, 47, 73, 82, 84, 86,130, 154* National Trust for Scotland and *38, 39, 44T, 45, 85T,* (NTS /Joe Rock); *43T* Museums of Scotland; *43B, 44B, 134, 135, 136* Glasgow Museums and Galleries; *83* New Town Conservation Committee. Contemporary illustrations from the NMR archive originate from Moubray House Press (Douglas McGregor) with the following exceptions: *18* and *46* (Eric Ellington), *50, 51, 72,* (Nic Allen).

Reproduction by Centre Graphics Limited, Livingston.
Printed in Scotland for HMSO by (13218)
Dd. 293035 C30 9/95

FOREWORD

One recompense for the long nights of the Scottish winter is the chance for the passer-by in a city street to glimpse the fluorescent-lit interiors of offices occupying the former town houses of the Georgian and Victorian upper classes. But, although the lack of curtains may be welcome for allowing sight of an enriched plaster ceiling or massive carved chimneypiece, the office workers' computer screens seem at odds with a setting which almost proclaims that it was intended for pleasure not business. Unfortunately for the curious outsider, the occupants of the huge majority of houses still in domestic use draw their curtains or close their shutters when darkness falls.

A longing to get inside other people's houses is so widely shared a human phenomenon that it cannot be explained in terms of aesthetic awareness. It is much more to do with the realisation, even if unconscious, that the interior of a house reveals a huge amount about its owner's preoccupations, aspirations and sense of status, as well as taste. But people's concerns vary from country to country and from century to century. To look inside Scottish houses built since the Renaissance, which are described and illustrated in *Behind the Façade*, is to witness the changing nature of Scottish society during the past four hundred years and to see how its members' changing preoccupations have brought about the construction of new houses and the alteration of existing ones. But is all change? There remains the question, perhaps only to be answered by a foreigner, of whether an obdurate national character can be found in the great variety of Scottish interiors produced over the centuries. The question it may be wiser not to ask is whether such a national character, if identified, would be recognised by the present Scottish occupants of these interiors.

John Gifford

John Gifford
The Buildings of Scotland

Atlas supports the world above the porch of Cardy House in
Fife, built by descendants of Alexander Selkirk, the castaway
who was the inspiration for Daniel Defoe's *Robinson Crusoe*.

ACKNOWLEDGEMENTS

I am grateful to the publishers, HMSO, and most particularly to Alastair Fyfe Holmes, the Scottish Publishing Manager, who recognised the potential for this volume which contains some of the best and most comprehensive photographs ever taken of Scottish domestic interiors. Several houses are documented for the first time in book form, including Mount Stuart, the thatched croft, Cardy House and the Glasgow West End house. Without the generous co-operation of the Royal Commission on the Ancient and Historical Monuments of Scotland and the National Monuments Record of Scotland, from whose archive most of the photographs were selected, this book would not have been possible. In addition, I acknowledge the contribution of Ian Gow, who has unstintingly shared his knowledge and wit in the interpretations of photographs from the archive which are included here. John Gifford, editor of *Buildings of Scotland*, too, has generously contributed scholarly commentaries, laced with his inimitable *esprit*, particularly on the interiors of classical Edinburgh and of Manderston, Berwickshire and on the subject of laird's halls. Ian Gow and John Gifford acted as consultant editors to the *Scottish Interiors* series which inspired this book. My thanks, too, to Dorothy Bosomworth, Roger Billcliffe, Margaret Swain, Victor Chinnery, John MacLean, Michael Donnelly, the late Colin McWilliam, Nicolas Allen, Fay Young and Jeremy Bruce-Watt, all of whom contributed to the original *Scottish Interiors* series. Many of the contemporary interiors illustrated in the book were photographed by Douglas McGregor under contract to Moubray House Press. These, and other original negatives, are now held in the collection of the National Monuments Record of Scotland. The participation of the owners of the houses featured in this book has been vital, of course, in the representation of a broad cross-section of interiors. In 1986–7 several owners opened their doors to writer and camera for the first time and revealed their devotion to preserving and enhancing the fabric and interiors of their historic charge, however demanding the challenge in terms of time and finance. They included John Noble of Ardkinglas, David Liddell-Grainger of Ayton, Ivy Jardine, formerly of Cardy House, Nick and Limma Groves-Raines, formerly of Peffermill House, Marc and Karen Ellington of Towie Barclay, Adrian Palmer of Manderston and residents of the New Town of Edinburgh. Thanks, too, to Keith and Liz Adam of Blairadam, Lady Dunpark, and Flora Maxwell Stuart of Traquair House. Sadly, five owners have died since the original photographs were taken and it is my hope that their families and friends will regard the book as a tribute to John, 6th Marquis of Bute, Jack Howells and John Pinkerton, Donald Mackenzie and Willie Maclaren.

Diana and her Nymphs by Robert Burns (1869-1941), designed for Crawford's Tea Rooms, Edinburgh's Art Nouveau equivalent of Charles Rennie Mackintosh's Willow Tea Rooms in Glasgow.

CONTENTS

RENAISSANCE YEARS
1560–1700

'A delictible tyme of peax'

The inscription over the entrance lintel
at Northfield House reads 'Except the
Lord Bulds in Vane Bulds Man'

Interior decorative painting was all the rage between 1580 and 1650. Exuberant painted ceilings enriched the homes of nobles, lairds, merchants and craftsmen throughout Renaissance Scotland. Their composition was 'unaturall or unworldly . . . for delight sake of man' wrote Henry Peacham in *The Art of Drawing* (1606): 'You may, if you list, draw naked boyses riding or playing with their paper-mills or bubble-shells upon Grates, Eagles, Dolphins, etc. the bones of a Rammes head hung with strings of beads, with Ribands, Satyres, Tritons, apes, cornucopias . . . cherries and any other inuention with a thousand more such idle toyes, so that herein you cannot be too fantastical'. Patrons of the art included establishment figures like the Marquis of Huntly who commissioned an emblematic ceiling and chapel painted with sacred subjects, merchants like Sir George Bruce of Culross Palace where there were once eight painted rooms, and the tenant of Sailors' Walk, Kirkcaldy where the beams of the old house overlooking the harbour displayed painted texts including: 'They that go down to the sea in ships, that do businesse in great waters. These see the works of the Lord and his wonders in the deep.'

The proprietors of Renaissance Scotland looked to the heavens for guidance about the organisation of society, to flora, fauna, myths and biblical stories for the design of their textiles, embroideries and painted decorations, and to the landscape and the structures of their ancestors for their architectural forms. Their ebullient sense of the divine related to the sacred space of their homes and surrounding garden ground and landscape. Visitors crossing the threshold first doffed their caps and bowed their heads under stone lintels inscribed with mottos like 'Lvfe God Abvfe Al and Yi Nychbovr As Yi Self', 'The Feir of the Lord Preserveth the Lyfe' and 'Blessit be God for all his Giftis'. They wended their way up spiral staircases and into the interiors of the towerhouse homes and tenements of that golden age of prosperity, before the Act of Union, which far from being dark and dour, rejoiced in colour, texture and design.

These evocative towerhouses had no parallel elsewhere in Europe (except, perhaps, the Irish variant) and remain Scotland's finest contribution to the architectural heritage of Europe. And although European influences inspired the vivacious interior decoration of painted ceilings and walls, embroidered hangings and other artifacts, their translation within the privileged Renaissance home was unique. The 'long sixteenth century' produced a new class, 'the middling sort', as well as a population boom which, despite plagues and famines, intensified the vulnerability of the poor and increased the divide between rich and poor. The 'homes' of the disenfranchised were but the temporary shelters of abject lives.

The towerhouses and mansions of the privileged were architectural microcosms which elevated the ancient broch or dun into grander constructions, defensive at first, encapsulated within thick stone walls. The blueprints for these structures had evolved from earlier, fortified castles and keeps like Dirleton, Borthwick and Glamis: architectural forms which had emanated, in turn, mostly from the inherited memory of stonemasons casting back 2000 years to the structures of their ancestors. The broch, too, was a uniquely Scottish architectural form of, above ground level, a double-skin stone wall, its hollow interior used for storage at the first floor, and the living accommodation in wooden structures erected against the stone wall and ringing the courtyard's central hearth. And these fortified dwellings, now dimly recalled, translated well enough to the defended residences of the rulers of the land and their retinues, from Inverness to Argyll, who had kingdoms to protect.

A great medieval household on the move, such as that of James IV moving across the Peeblesshire hills from the hunting lodge in the Yarrow Valley to Neidpath Castle and on to the Palace of Holyroodhouse, formed an impressive procession of up to several hundred members, the important mounted and decorative, with cooks, scullions and their children following on foot and packhorses 'slipping and stumbling beneath their monstrous burdens' as Mark Girouard describes. 'These, when unpacked at the other end, would disgorge plate, jewels, tapestries, table-cloths, clothing, hangings, coffers, musical instruments, carpenter's tools, mass-books, mass-vessels, vestments, linen, pots and pans, cooking-spits, and beds by the dozen. A household on the move was like a tortoise without the shell. The shell, or rather the shells, stood scattered ten, twenty, or several hundred miles apart, in the form of castles, manors and lodges belonging to the lord of the household.' The arrival of the household brought the structures to life as the rooms filled with people and their goods and gear.

Britain, on the outskirts of civilization, had drawn on the architectural influences and inspiration of the rich and populous continent of medieval Europe since the twelfth century. Castles and smaller fortified residences, though, always had a strong national character and were still made of timber around 1300, with a few exceptions whose policies included high towered walls, triangular, rectangular or polygonal according to the landscape of the site. In addition to fortifications, a medieval castle would usually embrace a substantial house for the lord or keeper, with its own private hall, usually at first floor level, a communal great hall of stone or wood and additional wooden buildings for domestic accommodation scattered within the bailey. Compact single stone towers or 'fortalices' with small courts or 'barmkins' enclosed within a wall with a ditch beyond, served as typical laird's homes, as at Traquair, throughout the fourteenth century

Those who had accepted land, power and wealth also accepted obligations: to administer local government, raise fighting men for the army or 'host' or for local skirmishes, and maintain courtly ceremony. They were responsible for large households of people from all walks of life which revolved around the heart of the castle: the great hall which is thought to have derived from the Norse long house or 'firehouse', similar to the Bu, (probably a drinking hall) at the Earl's Palace near Orphir in Orkney, whose foundations are still visible.

By the reign of James VI the medieval castle which households moved to and from, frequently for defensive reasons, had evolved into the settled country house. Strong central government had gradually displaced the need for landlords to retain defensive strongholds and the onerous obligations that went with them. The new houses incorporated concepts like comfort and privacy for the first time. Their walls were designed to ward off uninvited intruders rather than to signal readiness for attack. But some were slow to leave 'the great stone shells built in an earlier age'. The Countess of Angus remained, tortoise-like, in the noble residence of Bothwell Castle, the Earl of Argyll held to his castles at Dunstaffnage and Skipness, and the Earl of Atholl to Balvenie, while lesser lairds constructed towerhouse gems like Claypotts, Carsluith, Tolquhon and Aboyne, and merchants developed townhouses like Gladstane's Land and Provand's Lordship and tenements like John Knox House and Moubray House.

Although the more-or-less settled world of Renaissance Scotland no longer required the fortified castle-broch blueprint, the basic form translated well to the domestic towerhouse and its offspring tenements which the new class of lairds and merchants began to build everywhere. Individual variations, of L -, Z -, T - or E - plans, were developed from simple rectangles according to the requirements of the owner or family: harled stone towers, pitched roofs, sometimes carried on barrel vaults, with 'corbie' or 'crowstep' gables, crenellated and corbelled parapets. Angle turrets or 'bartizans', borrowed from the French, lent a peculiar character to the nationally flowering towerhouse style and throughout the sixteenth and seventeenth centuries the form became more elaborate with, for example, the provision of additional minor rooms, well lit by natural light, while modest dwellings and mansions, where the first floor hall was the important room, changed little.

These buildings were Renaissance Scotland's ideal homes, attuned to landscape and climate, in which the vertical, fortified forms of the ancestors lingered on, signalling aspiration to power, wealth, status and divine approbation. The Heracletian maxim: 'As Above, So Below', still governed the organisation of the early Renaissance world. The hierarchy of the household, with noble or laird at its head, was seen as a reflection of the macrocosm with God at its head and centre. Similarly, the hierarchy of society with the monarch at its head was God-given, and based on the natural order ruled over by God, in which man was but a microcosm of the universe, his animal passions subject to his will.

But as the seventeenth century progressed, the size and layout of the rooms made it possible for the head of the household and his family increasingly to separate themselves from their servants. The standing and position of the owner was reflected in the complexity of his building: the higher his station the larger his household, and the more plentiful the provision of halls, chambers, lodgings and service accommodation. Public rooms were lit by larger windows and private chambers 'ceased to be pokey little closets carved out of the castle walls' as David Breeze observes, but were of good size and interior design. The Renaissance rooms at Newark Castle (1599) still retain the painted ceiling, pine-panelled walls, fireplace, toilet-closet and characteristic bed recess or box-bed described by a visitor to Scotland in 1598: 'their bedsteds were then like cubbards in the wall, with doores to be opened and shut at pleasure, so as we climbed up to our beds'.

Inspired by mason-architects imbued with their patrons' love of display, each building exhibited both common components and unique vernacular inspiration. Teamwork was involved. The financial and administrative aspects of constructing a building were dealt with by masters of works, and master masons and master wrights were probably mainly responsible for the design. However, as John Gifford points out, someone who acted regularly as a master of works on buildings was almost bound to develop opinions about architecture, and William Schaw (d.1602), whose tombstone describes him as the 'king's architect', was one. Although the first use of the term 'architect' refers to Schaw, a landed gentleman appointed as master of works in 1583, no designs have been firmly ascribed to him, and Alexander Seton, 1st Earl of Dunfermline, for whom Schaw worked, is known to have had a knowledge of architecture. James Murray, a craftsman, was later a master of works, too, and became king's architect in 1612. And John Mylne (1611–1667), architect of the Tron Kirk in Edinburgh, followed a familial line of royal master masons going back to the fifteenth century, becoming both royal architect and practical craftsman. By the late seventeenth century all master masons had to show that they could design a building, and a distinction emerged at this time between amateur or gentlemen architects who could produce design plans but not necessarily make a building stand up, and mason-architects or craftsmen-architects who could both construct and design. Master masons who were not royal officials joined the ranks of craftsmen-architects. Tobias Bauchope was a craftsman-architect who worked as a builder for Sir William Bruce (c.1630–1710), a politician and amateur architect.

For several decades intellectuals had recognised that the Church in Scotland needed reform. William Dunbar and Sir David Lindsay had lambasted its malpractices, the latter uncompromisingly so in *Ane Satyre of the Thrie Estaitis*. In 1559 John Knox helped to draw up the first *Book of Discipline*, with its suggestions for religious and educational reform, six years after the last performance of *Ane Satyre* had been put on at the foot of the Calton Hill in Edinburgh. Mary, Queen of Scots, returned to Scotland as Catholic queen of a Protestant country reformed by the European doctrines of Calvin and

Luther with its own Confession of Faith. The Reformation abolished the authority of the Pope and made the celebration of Mass an offence, and the reformers banned processions and carnivals. But Mary revived music at Holyrood, deer ran in its park once more and the royal library swelled with books from all over Europe. Her traumatic reign was dominated by the warring factions of religions rather than armies and it was not until after the interregnum of the Regencies, when James VI assumed direct government in 1587, that fear of attack receded. By 1622 Scotland was enjoying what his Privy Council described as a 'delictible tyme of peax under your majesteis regne'. Peace brought relative prosperity, and the domestic architecture of Scotland assumed a gallant and evolving national identity throughout the seventeenth century when two new professions, the law and the ministry, emerged. The rise of 'the middling sort', included the likes of William Forbes of Menie, who completed the building of Craigievar (1626) from a fortune made trading in the Baltic, lairds like Edward Edgar who built Peffermill House (1636) and Sir Patrick Barclay who expanded the 'castell' at Towie into a fine house, reflecting the age in an enigmatic inscription above the new front door: 'In tym of valth al men seemis frindly ane frind is not knavin but in adversitie'.

It was as if a full orchestra of mastercraftsmen pooled memory, skill and materials in a glorious celebration of palace houses, towerhouses, townhouses and tenements in Scotland's first building boom. Domestic comfort was the priority as defensive structures were gradually modified or replaced. What had been the lord's or keeper's house in a castle became the model for the towerhouse, which had no need of fortifications. The great communal hall became obsolete since there were no troops of armed knights to support, and the first-floor hall, the lord's hall, sometimes 100 feet long, evolved from the model of the private hall in the fortified lord's house and grand houses included a long gallery in the French style. Although the great hall, originally within the walls of a fortified structure, disappeared, the term 'great hall' is still used, for example by The National Trust for Scotland, to describe what is, in fact, the lord's hall. Thus the term 'great hall' is common in, for example, descriptions of its properties, but the reader should be aware that 'hall' is the correct usage.

Now privileged lairds and merchants enjoyed what were effectively the first country houses, with home a delightful retreat. Vaulted basements housed the fiery kitchens below the earthly paradise of the hall, a communal room of distinction and conviviality where vivid ceilings married heaven to earth in a glorious painted cacophony of motifs inspired by the galaxy and the natural world, mythology and biblical stories. In the wake of the Protestant Reformation, alliances were formed or revitalised with England, the Scandinavian countries and the vibrant young Dutch republic whose artifacts, from ceramics to painted ceilings and maps, influenced interior decoration. Manifestations of a vigorous trading network with France as well as the Baltic and the Low Countries, now infiltrated many strands of life including the decoration of homes. And visitors looking though ventilation shutters under glazed windows into these rooms, would have discovered interiors filled with colour, texture and design. The late twentieth-century investigator, unable to time travel, is left to create a virtual reality by visiting the wealth of Renaissance houses open to the public and assembling facts and hints handed on by historians who have studied archival documents, including house inventories and contemporary artifacts.

Traquair House, the Borders towerhouse where Stewart descendants still live and said to be the oldest inhabited house in Scotland, is a fine place to begin such a journey. And the Palaces of Holyroodhouse, Stirling and Falkland and the grand homes of Burnett of Crathes and Forbes of Craigievar, reveal to us the *ne plus ultra* of Renaissance interiors. But more modest surviving examples within mixed communities help to broaden our imaginative reconstruction of Renaissance housing stock. Edinburgh's Royal Mile contains some of the best examples in Britain, built for nobles associated with Holyroodhouse and the castle and for merchants of the Royal Burgh. An address list includes the tenements of John Knox House, Moubray House and Gladstane's Land, and townhouses like Acheson House and Tweeddale House; while, across the Firth of Forth, the evolution of Culross Palace within the extraordinary town of Culross reflects the rise in status and fortune of George Bruce who built it. It is a nobleman's house, funded by collieries and trade. By the end of the sixteenth century merchants and landowners were amassing fortunes from the boom in overseas trade. Baronial houses for the new 'middling sort' like Towie Barclay and Craigievar remain to symbolise the age while, on the other hand, monuments to its urban and rural poor, if any such monuments existed, have been swept away by time. 'Their experience,' comments historian Michael Lynch, 'lies buried in the dry and often formidably complex statistics of mortality rates and subsistence crises, the likelihood of increasing mobility of population and evidence of a drastic fall in standards of diet.'

The evolution of Traquair House, from simple tower to near-palace, demonstrates the dramatic development of a grand house between the fifteenth and seventeenth centuries. Although at first glance Traquair House looks unadulterated, closer inspection reveals that it incorporates work of many different periods and has attained its present appearance only as a result of a long and complicated structural evolution though, fortunately, two sets of architectural plans for remodelling the façade in the seventeenth and eighteenth centuries were never instituted.

Originally a hunting lodge of considerbale antiquity, the property was granted to James Stewart, the first builder of Traquair. In 1492, he constructed his 'turris et fortalicium de Trakware' to be a small, free-standing towerhouse of three storeys with an attic. And although that construction was absorbed by later extensions, its ground-floor apartments still form the nucleus of the whole building. Varying wall alignments and thicknesses, as well as evidence from documentary material including the family archives, make it possible to trace the outline and form of James Stewart's 'turris'. But it was the developments of his Jacobite Catholic heirs throughout the sixteenth and seventeenth centuries that created the house's present archetypal appearance: a rectangular harled block with wings off, small irregularly disposed windows, steeply-pitched slate roofs and corbelled out maverick angle-turrets, carved windows with pistol-holes or peep-holes and three wide-mouthed gun-ports with inclined sills incorporated in the 1642 tower.

A century later, the 'turris et fortalicium' had expanded considerably with the addition of a south wing, incorporating a stair tower rising to the height of the original tower, and another wing to the south later with a window-lintel on the west front inscribed with the initials of Sir William Stewart, 5th of Traquair, 1599. By the seventeenth century the house was referred to as the 'Palace' of Traquair.

A substantial fragment of the original tower remains incorporated in the house: the northernmost cellar, which leads by means of a covered passage into the chapel, is the ground-floor apartment of the fifteenth-century tower from which the narrow original staircase rises within the wall thickness to the three upper floors. It was retained as a service wing after the mid-sixteenth-century wing, entered near its turnpike tower, was constructed. It is through this later wing that visitors have entered Traquair House ever since, and a later wrought-iron door-knocker is decorated with an earl's coronet, an intricate reversed monogram CSETMM for Charles Stewart, 4th Earl of Traquair and his wife Mary Maxwell, with the date 1705. The turnpike stair still provides the main access to the upper floors above a circular-headed door frame carved with fleur-de-lis spandrels, a scene of a unicorn goring a lion, both standing on an elephant bearing a howdah, and the date 1601. A lobby on the south side contains barrel-vaulted cellars, the original towerhouse stair and what might have been a prison.

Today's visitors trace the same sixteenth century approach to the first-floor suite of three rooms, the principal apartments, which remain much as they were when altered by Edinburgh architect James Smith around 1700. The King's Room panelling properly belongs to the end of the Renaissance but an earlier roll-and-hollow moulded fireplace, a 'Hollandia' scene on a cast-iron fireback, and original garderobes in the angle of the original towerhouse sit well with a fine *lit de parade*. The adjacent apartment displays similar features with a concealed cupboard in the panelling near the fireplace. Since originally it functioned as the High Dining Room, the High Drawing Room is the most lavishly decorated apartment in the house. The elaborate panelling with fluted composite pilasters, matching doors with lug-moulded architraves and an alcove formed between a corner cupboard and entrance vestibule are all Smith's work.

Traquair was well endowed with painted decoration. In 1954, an early scheme came to light when portions of a timber ceiling were discovered under a later plaster ceiling. Sections of this late sixteenth-century work can be seen by visitors to the house.

It was a beam-and-board ceiling but the boards had been removed and the remaining wood was decorated in tempera, the soffits with running arabesque designs and the side panels with scriptural texts in Gothic letters within interlacing borders. The colours used were brown, ochre, white, green and orange inscribed in black punctuated with red, and the texts were taken from the 1560 Geneva version of the Bible, varied by the painter when necessary to fit the space available on the wood. The vernacular spelling of the texts suggests that the painter did not work directly from the printed source but had memorised the verses. Ceilings with similar decoration exist at Nunraw, East Lothian, Collairnie Castle, Fife, and Delgatie Castle, Abderdeenshire. Lord Traquair's Room and the Tailor's Room in the south portion of the main block both contain seventeenth-century features: panelling, fireplaces, doorways and entablature with triglyphic friezes. In 1965, traces of painted decoration were discovered on the wall-surface behind the panelling in the Tailor's Room, probably from 1599. The painting was well-preserved tempera: black, grey, gold, red and blue. The celestial theme, a *trompe l'oeil* composition of clouds, stars, and new moon, may have been associated with a painted ceiling depicting the seasons or classical deities.

What is now the museum was originally two small apartments. An abrupt change in the thickness of the west and east walls marks the south wall of the original towerhouse, removed around the middle of the sixteenth century, leaving one room which contains relics of a garderobe and a sixteenth-century fireplace. And around 1880 a remarkable mural painting came to light on the south wall which may have been one of a series that ran round the room. The decoration is executed in black, yellow and red tempera on plaster and depicts vines, birds including an eagle, a collared hound, a squirrel, a galloping Bactrian camel and a painted border top and bottom of scriptural texts in Gothic lettering. Like the High Drawing Room paintings, the texts derive from the Geneva Bible.

The Stewarts of Traquair were among the élite of Scotland who had related to Edinburgh as the capital ever since Robert I granted it a royal charter in 1329; by the fifteenth century it had become a bustling town where the Stewart kings made their royal residence in Edinburgh Castle and the present Old Town had assumed its pattern within the city walls. Throughout the land, in urban towerhouses or mansions surrounded by garden ground, and in the top floor apartments of tenemented townhouses, all but the poor lived as far away as possible from the unspeakable, rotting stench of the streets, closes, pends and wynds. There the poor subsisted in hovels or thatched wooden lean-tos attached to established buildings. The foul cities were rife with disease, violence and other crimes, and, as is well known, refuse, including sewage, was deposited in the streets.

The historian Hector Boece described sixteenth-century courtly and mercantile Edinburgh as excelling in 'polese, reparation, wisdome and riches'. On the other hand, the city's first poet, William Dunbar, lambasted the council and the Court of Session for tolerating the miserable living conditions of commoners, the swindling tactics of merchants and the hypocrisy of the Church. The gulf between rich and poor was, declaimed Dunbar, a cause for 'schame':

> *For stink of haddockis and of scattis,*
> *For cryis of carlingis and debattis,*
> *For fensum flyttingis of defame;*
> *Think ye not schame,*
> *Before strangeris of all estaittis*
> *That sic dishonour hurt your name!*

In mid-sixteenth-century Aberdeen, however, Gordon of Rothiemay found buildings of stone and lime, roofed in slate, of three or four stories high, with adjoining orchards and gardens: 'the dwelling houses are cleanlie and bewtifull and neat, both within and without, and the syde that looks to the street mostlie adorned with galleries of timber, which they call forestaires'.

Towerhouses peppered the landscape beyond Edinburgh as in Aberdeen, Glasgow and other emerging towns, and a considerable number were built within the city walls themselves. Tweeddale House, a small tower in the Royal Mile, built by Neil Laing, Keeper of the Signet, was expanded by his son John in 1602 to be a 'dwelling hous'. And in the 'heich hoose' of Moubray House, an early tenement of two houses and luckenbooth, Scotland's first portrait painter George Jamesone took up tenancy in 1635. Jamesone's first association with Edinburgh had been in 1612 when he arrived from Aberdeen to be apprenticed to John Anderson, 'pictor' and guild burgess of Aberdeen. Anderson was a decorator-cum-artist working with other recorded painters on the interior decorative painting of country houses in the Lowlands. But as soon as his apprenticeship ended in 1620 Jamesone's career as a portrait painter began, with a study of Paul Menzies, later provost of Aberdeen. Early title deeds describe his co-tenants in the 'heich hoose' tenement of Moubray House as an armourer, a carver and a glasswright. The 1637–40 *Self-portrait in a Room* symbolically depicts a piece of armour, an hour-glass, carved wood as well as a skeletal *memento mori,* and an array of Jamesone's own paintings, including a *Chastisement of Cupid,* which would seem to fix the scene within Moubray House.

The Jamesone portrait of Anne Erskine and her daughters is one of the earliest paintings to show an interior view. A group of portraits 'of a distinctly Jamesone type' surrounds a larger painting similar to the *Chastisement of Cupid* in his self-portrait, hinting that the room was the gallery of the house. During the sixteenth century the fashion for collecting portraits in grand houses developed apace. The portraits depicted present royalty, ancient emperors, ancestors, relations and the great and good of the day. James VI, whom the poet, Alexander Montgomerie, of the Renaissance court's 'Castilian

Band', dubbed the 'Royal Apollo', was also represented as Solomon, Augustus, Brutus, Arthur, Constantine and David in portraits of the day. The fashion, no doubt, provided a demand for Jamesone's prodigious output and played a part in Jamesone's rise to fame as a portrait painter, the 'Scottish Van Dyck' who became something of legend even in his own day. The recessed mullion window is Dutch in style, the table is covered with a red fringed cloth which seems to match a draped curtain which softens an otherwise sparse corner of the room, and a trinket box presumably symbolises the countess's wealth. The group stands on a floor of greenish-black and ochre tiles.

The hall, ubiquitous feature of medieval fortified dwellings and the place for 'large tabling and belly cheer', remained the focus of Renaissance homes like the Erskines', and contained the largest piece of furniture in the house, the communal table or 'hie burde'. The long, communal dining table is thought to have inspired the rectangular layout of the hall. To signify the hall's importance, decorative plasterwork on stone vaults and overmantels, or painted work, embellished the stone hearth of the hall where fires provided comfort. Decorative plasterwork was undertaken by journeymen plasterers who, like the decorative painters, travelled widely in the seventeenth century. In wealthy homes the chimney opening was provided with a carved fire-surround and surmounted with a stone, plaster or wooden overmantel, often charged with the arms of the family. The heraldry above the massive granite lintel of the fireplace in the hall at Craigievar is one of the most magnificent examples of early plasterwork in Britain. The moulds used at Craigievar were also used at Bromley-by-Bow in 1606, Glamis in 1620 and Muchalls in 1624. The arms of William Forbes and his wife Margaret Woodward appear on either side of the central pendant. As tenant-in-chief of the Crown, the laird of Craigievar was entitled to display his achievement and his authority to administer justice over his lands in the king's name at barony courts. According to Victor Chinnery, author of *Oak Furniture: The British Tradition,* most Renaissance houses contained a range of furniture: the large table or 'hie burde', a serving table, chairs, stools or backstools, chests for storage, at least one cupboard and beds. Inventories of the period refer to chests placed 'at the bed's feet' for the safe storage of valuables, or 'at the stairshead'. Newly finished oak furniture and woodwork, though, is a pale biscuit colour and not the dark, richly patinated wood of surviving examples, and, as Victor Chinnery points out, it is important to remember that, while admiring the softening and darkening effect of age, the furniture of a reconstructed room of the period rarely gives a true impression of its original appearance.

Furniture in Glasgow's Burrell Collection and Provand's Lordship, offer sturdy reminders that Renaissance landowners and burghers appreciated the highest standards of craftsmanship. But where did their furniture come from? There were probably several centres of furniture-making in Renaissance Scotland. The eastern seaports Leith, Dundee, Montrose and Aberdeen, supported thriving mercantile communities and the furniture produced in these centres is still found scattered in country houses and castles. Cultural contacts between France and Scotland around the time of Mary, Queen of Scots, inspired a penchant for *caqueteuse* armchairs, chairs to 'cackle' or gossip in. These fine examples of Franco-Scottish design are principally associated with the urban workshops of Aberdeen and Edinburgh. Nuances of individual local styles such as simple jointed armchairs of oak and pine are beginning to be analysed. David Jones, for example, has identified a clear Fife regional style. Furniture such as a pine chair from Stonehaven and another from Lumphanan, dated 1688, suggests a vivid but robust tradition of manufacture in the countryside and fishing ports using local woods.

Aberdeen was rich and influential at the beginning of the seventeenth century. The city housed one of the four universities and served a large hinterland peppered with towerhouses in the north-east. At Trinity Hall, headquarters of the Incorporated Trades of Aberdeen, a group of *caqueteuse* chairs was assembled in the seventeenth century which represent the finest products then available in the city. The guild organisations comprised hammermen, bakers, wrights and coopers, barber surgeons, tailors, shoemakers, weavers and fleshers. The chairs were donated to mark their terms of office by deacons of each trade, or by the master of the company. An inventory of 1696 lists a total of twenty-three *caqueteuse* chairs or box-base armchairs, fifteen of which can still be identified.

The examples below include Andrew Watson's *caqueteuse* chair which is probably the earliest dated piece of mahogany of British make (1661), though Victor Chinnery recently discovered an undated chair in Brazilian mahogany or bulletwood which appears to have been made for the Roope family of Dartmouth around 1617.

Hammermen
ane cheer gifted by Matthew Guild, armourer.
ane cheer gifted by Patrick Whyt, bookmaker,
Deacon Conveener, 1690

Wrights and Coopers
ane cheer gifted by Jerome Blak, couper, 1574
ane cheer gifted by William Ord, wright,
Deacon Conveener, 1635

Taylziours
ane cheer gifted by Thomas Cordyn, tayler,
Deacon Conveener, 1627

Fleshers
ane cheer gifted by Andrew Watson, Deacon
ane cheer marked WP coft to the Hospital

The timber of Andrew Watson's mahogany chair is extremely close-grained, hard and of a reddish hue with bright patination. Over the years it has undergone good polishing with slight but even wear. Mahogany, 'Spanish' or 'Jamaica' wood, was well known by the middle of the seventeenth century and a few planks might well have come in through the busy port of Aberdeen from Spain or France. But oak and pine are the usual furniture timbers, whether native or imported from Scandinavia like the pine planks for ceiling and panelling.

The Long Gallery at Crathes has a rare oak-panelled ceiling with finely cut panels overlaid with a pattern of moulded ribs in diamond and oblong formations. The ribs are punctuated by coats of arms and recurrent motifs of the holly leaf emblem of the founding Burnett family, and the Horn of Leys. The centre rib displays six shields belonging to the first baronet: the King of Scotland, his overlord, the Marquis of Hamilton, his cousin, Lord Dunfermline, the Chancellor of Scotland and a close friend, Alexander Burnett, his great-grandfather, and Gilbert Burnett, Bishop of Salisbury. But most of the ceilings were painted in the mid-Renaissance period.

Painted ceilings survive everywhere, but particular concentrations have been noted in the east where large groups of decorative painters may have formed 'schools' in Aberdeen and Edinburgh. The painters remain largely anonymous with a few exceptions. They were Scots who often worked in family groups, like the Binnings and Workmans of Edinburgh who passed their skills on from father to son. Stylistic similarities suggest that an artist or group of artists worked over a wide area. Ceilings as far apart as Culross and Burntisland in Fife and Cullen House in Banffshire, and Moubray House and Grandtully Chapel in Perthshire, for example, suggest the same hand. John Mellin has been linked with the ceilings at Delgatie Castle, Aberdeenshire, James Workman with Rossend and John Anderson with the decoration of the room in Edinburgh Castle where James VI is said to have been born. It was out of this background of decorative painting that Anderson's famous pupil, George Jamesone, emerged to become the leading portrait painter of the day.

In *Painted Ceilings of Scotland*, M. R. Apted suggests that the subject matter of a ceiling was governed by the taste of the patron or the ability and imagination of the painter. The decorators used a distemper-like paint produced from a mixture of pigments and glue size, covered the ceiling with a thin coat of whiting and laid down the pattern, frequently within a geometric grid. It is impossible to pull out any unifying philosophical thread as Duncan Thomson, Keeper of the National Portrait Gallery, observes in *Painting in Scotland 1570–1650*. 'However, the meaning of each individual emblem was probably well enough known since they had had a wide currency in Europe since the fifteenth century, although the origin of many was medieval or classical . . . engraved and printed material circulated widely, editions of the same book appearing in a number of cities at different times, often using the same blocks, and the emblem books became a common source of decorative imagery.' Emblem books which influenced the decorative painters include Claude Paradin's *Symbola Heroica* (1583), Geoffrey Whitney's *A Choice of Emblemes, and other Devises* (1586). Conrad Gesner's two volumes, *Historiae Animalium* (1551) and *Icones Animalium* (1560), inspired the porcupine and the rhinoceros on the painted ceiling at Rossend Castle and many other animals on the ceilings. Celtic sources also appear in the form of heraldic motifs and patterns at Huntingtower Castle and St Mary's, Grandtully, for example. The painters adjusted the design to fit the structure, most frequently simple beam-and-board ceilings like those which survive at Northfield and Crathes. Grander constructions in which the timbers were used to create covered, elliptical or barrel-vaulted ceilings, suspended or supported within the roof space, provided a large area for the artist's creation, free from the confines of beam-and-board.

Why were painted ceilings rare in England, except for the north, yet common in Scotland? The Lowland shortage of timber led to the importation of Scandinavian and Baltic softwoods in the sixteenth century, but these lacked the aesthetic quality of English hardwoods and required enhancing. It seems reasonable to suppose that the Continental penchant for ceiling painting could have been imported along with the wood itself. Painting was the easiest and most cost-effective way to express exuberant display and to communicate the important symbols of the household. The colourful confidence of such ceilings must also have appealed as an appropriate outward expression of a nation enjoying a period of new prosperity, new learning and the strengthening of its alliances with Scandinavia, the Baltic and Holland.

A slow process of detective work and discovery over the past fifty years, led by Stenhouse Conservation Centre, has revealed the extraordinary variety and geographic spread of Renaissance interior painting: from the purely classical celestial ceilings of Mary Somerville's House in Fife and Cullen House, Banffshire (tragically destroyed by fire in June 1987) to the *trompe l'oeil* effects at Pinkie House, Musselburgh, and the occult symbolism of Preston Grange in East Lothian. Although each ceiling is unique, all share an uninhibited love of colourful decoration and similarity of style and technique. Above all, they demonstrate the use of classical content and decorative detail for the first time in Scottish iconography. Secular imagery is far more common than Christian symbolism in these art works of the post-Reformation, which characterise, more than any other contemporary painting, an age of vision, change and incongruity.

The earliest known painted ceiling, showing the date 1581, was discovered at Preston Grange in 1962, less than a mile from Northfield whose owner, Schomberg Scott, freed that house's glorious Renaissance art from its Georgian plasterwork shield in the 1950s. Almost four hundred years of darkness had kept the design as bright as on the day it was finished at the beginning of the seventeenth century. The Northfield ceiling remains *in situ*, zealously protected by Schomberg Scott, while the Preston Grange ceiling, removed for safe-keeping to Merchiston Castle in recent times, has lost its power of association with place forever. The ceiling is contemporary with the infamous 1580s witch trials at North Berwick, not far from Preston Grange, but the source of the designs is a work by François Rabelais, published in 1565 and not obviously associated with witchcraft. The country experienced what amounted to witch mania in the sixteenth century, as records of witch belief and contemporary accounts of meetings with fairies, or initiates of the witch cult relate. Calvinism, which held sin and the power of the devil to be terrible realities, undoubtedly fuelled the flames of witch belief which took hold in a more fanatical form in Scotland than in England.

Original painted ceilings are still being discovered and recreated. In the last few years, Stenhouse Conservation Centre, in whose hands the maintenance and conservation of most painted ceilings lies, is frequently called in to investigate new discoveries. Stenhouse, which is part of the Scottish Development Department's Directorate of Historic Buildings and Monuments, documented a fragment of painted ceiling at Advocates' Close in Edinburgh's Old Town recently and completed painstaking work at Kinneil House, West Lothian, and St Mary's Church at Grandtully, Perthshire. As Rab Snowden, the principal conservator has said, the decorated ceilings may seem naïve when set beside the contemporary art of Rubens and Rembrandt, but they provide a fascinating insight into the cultural and aesthetic needs of the post-Reformation.

In addition to panelling and painting, Renaissance rooms were usually hung with fabrics to keep out winter draughts. Several embroidered panels depicting borage, tulips and other flowers were discovered recently at Traquair House. Carefully wrapped in paper and packed in wooden trunks, when they emerged their colours retained their original brightness, a vivid reminder that needlework provided colour and decoration in Renaissance interiors that were formerly imagined to be dour and bare.

Tapestries and embroidered cloths were also used for upholstery: long cushions to soften hard wooden benches and window-seats, hangings, bedcovers and window covers. Chairs and settles were plentifully supplied with turkeywork, needlework or even plain cloth cushions. Fine carpets covered tables and sideboards rather than floors. The most coveted draught-excluders were thick woollen tapestries imported from Flanders and known by the generic name of 'arras' after the Flemish town of their manufacture. Lighter materials were also used, including a cheaper form of painted or stained cloths, commonly referred to in British inventories. These imitated tapestry, depicted a similar range of subjects, and were sometimes called 'counterfeit arras'.

Since they were immovable and ephemeral, decorated wallpapers are rarely mentioned even in English house inventories. However, 'flock' wallpapers were introduced from the Netherlands in the late seventeenth century: glued paper dusted with powdered and coloured wool ends produced a pattern, with further detail added by stencil. Pictorial subjects were common, as were floral patterns based on contemporary needlework. Given strong trading links with France and Northern Europe, it is reasonable to assume that these papers found their way into wealthier homes as an alternative to painted decoration towards the end of the Renaissance period. But given the Scots' penchant for painted planks and bearing in mind the damp state of their winter homes, it is unlikely that these papers ever caught on.

Embroidered hangings decorated the most expensive items of furniture in a Renaissance home: the beds, and particularly the bed of the owner and his wife, an elaborate affair, on view for all to see. 'The pine or "firr" structure would probably have succumbed to woodworm long before the hangings needed replacing,' according to Margaret Swain, an authority on Scottish textiles and embroideries. An early representation of a bed appears in the painting, *The Annunciation*, by Hans Memling (*c.* 1430–94). Here is the Virgin's bed hung with red curtains, one looped up, with a narrow flat pelmet hiding the curtain rods. The tester is thought to be suspended from the ceiling rather than held up by posts at the corners, but the shape of the bed and its hangings remained remarkably unchanged from medieval times until the end of the seventeenth century.

'Children slept on truckle beds, servants on pallets, but the imposing four-posted bed in the chief bedroom was the stage upon which the drama of life and death took place,' says Margaret Swain. 'It was there that the mother, newly delivered from the perils of childbirth, received the congratulations of visitors; where sorrowing relatives took leave of the dying and where the corpse was laid out before the burial.'

The typical beds of palaces and tenements alike were furnished with enclosing curtains, tester and upper valance or 'pand' to hide the curtain rods. And, in inventories, 'Bed' or 'Bed furniture' referred to the hangings rather than the stand, which was usually hidden and ephemeral. A few examples survive, like Queen Mary's bed at Traquair and the restored laird's bed at Crathes, which display these features. Two mattresses were usual, one filled with straw, the other with feathers rested on a 'canvas bottom' or a 'lath bottom' of wood battens. The red damask bed in the Tapestry Room at Blair Castle still retains its canvas bottom with reinforced eyelets through which ropes were threaded to lash the canvas to the beams at the side, head and foot of the bed. In towerhouse or tenement where rooms opened into other rooms without the privacy of corridors, bed curtains were necessary for privacy as well as warmth. Margaret Swain has observed that 'London cloth' in red and green was listed in 1640 at Balloch (now Taymouth Castle) and in Edinburgh 'striped Musselburgh cloth' (a coarse woollen) is often recorded. More ostentatious beds were hung with velvet or silk, with embroidered designs on the pelmet and curtains. A number of narrow valances in tent stitch on canvas survive from Perthshire castles of the time, some with well-drawn figures depicting biblical or mythological scenes and figures wearing French costume fashionable during and shortly after the time of Mary, Queen of Scots.

From 1561 to 1568, when Mary was in Scotland, her upholsterers and embroiderers laboured to repair bed hangings and create new ones, sometimes given as wedding gifts to her ladies. Selected entries from the inventories of Mary, Queen of Scots, and her mother, Mary of Guise, describe the richly decorated beds at the royal palaces:

> *A bed of broderie work on four colours of satin, red,*
>   *blue, yellow and white*
> *A bed of crimson velvet embroidered with phoenixes and*
>   *tears* (the emblem of Mary of Guise)
> *A bed of black velvet embroidered with arms and spheres*
> *Another of brown velvet with applied gold and silver,*
>   *with ciphers and flowers embroidered in silk and gold*
> *Another with true lovers' knots and the Greek letters*
> (for Mary, Queen of Scots' husband, Francis II of France)

A bed repaired in 1619 for the visit of Mary's son, James VI and I, depicted the *Labour of Hercules* in embroidery and was later taken to Hampton Court where it remained until the time of Cromwell's Commonwealth. The larger houses of Scotland, too, displayed splendid and inventive examples of bed hangings. A set of three valances from the bed of Sir Colin Campbell of Glenorchy and his wife Katherine Ruthven, whom he married in 1550, can be seen at the Burrell Collection in Glasgow. These are embroidered in silk and display the Campbell arms. The shortest valance, for the foot of the bed, shows the husband's arms impaling the Ruthven arms with a true lovers' knot suspended from a ram's head. On either side of the arms is a lively representation of the *Temptation of Adam and Eve* and their expulsion from paradise.

Margaret Swain advocates caution in attributing certain embroideries to Mary, Queen of Scots, but William Drummond of Hawthornden decisively attributed an elaborate set of bedhangings, embellished with emblems, to the needle of the Queen. Although that work has disappeared, examples of embroidery worked while she was a prisoner in England survive at the Victoria and Albert Museum. These moving testimonies are small panels of canvas work, octagonal or cruciform in shape, worked in cross stitch with silk thread. Some have personal associations like the leaping dolphin, a visual pun for her first husband, the *Dauphin,* or eldest son of the King of France, as he was when Mary married him. Small panels like this were easy to work on a small frame that could be carried around. Single motifs of flowers, animals and insects were worked on canvas, then stiffened before being cut out and applied to hangings of velvet or silk or even re-mounted onto new material when the old wore out. A bed decorated like this can be seen at Scone Palace, its original red velvet faded to tawny.

The carpets of the sixteenth and seventeenth centuries were walked on as little as possible and treasured for their decorative qualities. The 1578 Sheffield Portrait of Mary, Queen of Scots, was painted during her captivity in England. The Queen is standing on a 'small pattern Holbein carpet'. In an early seventeenth-century portrait the 3rd Earl of Lothian stands on a Turkish-style carpet. Another portrait in the Palace of Holyroodhouse shows Lord Darnley's mother, the Countess of Lennox, on a Lotto rug. Valuable and colourful rugs like these provided artists with rich backgrounds for portraits of royal and titled Renaissance patrons and formal portraiture offers a rich source of information about Oriental carpets, and Ottoman carpets woven near Ushak in Turkey in particular, which were popular in Europe from the fifteenth to the seventeenth century.

Certain carpet types are named after the artist who favoured, or had access to, a particular design: 'small pattern Holbein', 'large pattern Holbein' and 'Lotto', are examples. But, warns rug specialist, John MacLean, this system of identification can mislead the unaware. Large pattern Holbein carpets, for example, appear in portraits painted long after the artist's death.

However, since Mary, Queen of Scots, was removed to England without any possessions it is likely that the carpet in the portrait belonged to her custodian for fifteen years, the Earl of Shrewsbury. Other evidence suggests that the portrait and several other versions of it were not painted until the early seventeenth century, perhaps as keepsakes commissioned for Mary's loyal supporters after her death. The Countess of Lennox, too, was in England, at her Temple Newsam estate, when the Holyroodhouse portrait was painted and the Lotto carpet might have belonged there or travelled with her from Scotland as part of her 'removing garderobe'.

In addition to the study of portraits, documents including wills and inventories will, hopefully, continue to provide a rich source of information about the Oriental carpet in Scotland, though on nothing like the scale of the royal inventories compiled on the death of Henry VIII in 1547 opened up by the Victoria and Albert Museum recently. One of the most interesting inventories discovered so far relates to Mary of Guise who possessed: 'Twa auld Tapies of Turquie worn away'. The inventory of the Royal Wardrobe and Jewelhouse of Mary, Queen of Scots, lists: 'saxteen turkie tapies contening sevin greit and nine small'. An inventory taken of the furnishings destroyed in the explosion which killed Lord Darnley at Kirk o' Field was presented to Mary for counter-signature and notes 'a little Turkie carpet and a chamber-pot'.

The 1620 Strathmore carpet in the collection of the National Museums of Scotland, is one of the earliest carpets known to have come from a Scottish house. The Duke of Buccleuch owned two others, dated 1584 and 1585, in addition to the Strathmore carpet, which was a table carpet. They were, however, woven near Norwich and are typical of the hand-knotted and piled English reproduction Turkeywork carpets with jute warps and wefts which grew in popularity throughout the seventeenth century.

Enlightened about the architecture and basic artifacts of the Renaissance, it becomes possible to strip away the accretions of subsequent generations and even to reconstruct ruins. By the twentieth century, the countryside was littered with derelict towerhouses, many of which would be still be ragged shells but for the efforts of private individuals who recognised their potential as fine family homes, like the Ellingtons of Towie Barclay and the Groves-Raines who restored the 'heich hoose' of Moubray House as well as Peffermill House. Many others, too, have attempted such reconstruction in recent decades when the rush to purchase and restore ruinous or decrepit towerhouses assumed an intensity reminiscent of the passionate building boom of the age in which these architectural gems were first created. Now Aga cookers send warmth through reclaimed kitchens, firms specialising in reproduction furniture recreate carved pieces for halls, and the waxed cloth jackets of self-made lairds hang nonchalantly beside reproduction chain-mail made in Germany and swords made in Toledo.

It is a cause for celebration that so many Renaissance buildings have been saved and recreated. Towie Barclay, for example, was an agricultural shed minus the top two storeys when Marc and Karen Ellington bought the castle in 1969: 'The first buildings at Towie were probably of wood set within a palisade which reinforced the natural defences of the site,' according to historian John Gifford. 'By 1559 there was a stone-built 'castell'. Some of its walls may be incorporated in the present house, created by the 17th Barclay laird, Sir Patrick after 1587. A master mason who had worked at Gight Castle nearby seems to have also worked on Sir Patrick's house: the same swastika mason's mark appears here and at Craig Castle and Delgatty. The mason created a solid L-shaped tower, domestic with a strongly defensive appearance. Wide-mouthed gunloops gaped through the ground floor walls but the larger first floor windows hint at comfort inside.'

The twentieth-century Ellingtons have restored the master mason's floors, added a tall caphouse within the Victorian parapet and pink-harled the rubble masonry which sets off the dressed stonework of windows and doors from which they might imagine how Sir Patrick Barclay would have greeted his visitors. Whether led into the house by a servant, a member of the family, or by the laird himself, the ownership of the castle was signalled immediately by the arms and initials carved on the boss above the thick ribs of the vestibule's groin vault. A tunnel-vaulted passage passes the kitchen (now with an Aga stove where the open fire would once have been) and the original wine cellar (converted to a dining room by the Ellingtons) and ends in a flight of four steps and the broad turnpike stair leading to the hall. 'Now, with the saltire flying from the battlements, the house looks as though it might be the stronghold of a feudal baron once more,' comments John Gifford, who turned off the road to Turriff to visit Towie Barclay recently.

Architects Nicholas and Limma Groves-Raines took on the fortified towerhouse of Peffermill in 1981. The challenges they faced and solutions they found in the earlier restoration at Moubray House, stood them in good stead as they approached their next challenge, a seventeenth-century laird's house whose stone entrance inscription declares 'God will provyd'.

'Exactly such as a child would build with cards,' said Sir Walter Scott of the shape of the 1830 Peffermill House, which he described as situated with outhouses and 'a gallant crop' of dandelions and thistles. He was inspired by its central stair tower and steep crowstepped gable to imagine the house as the seat of the Laird of Dumbiedykes in his Waverley Novel, *The Heart Of Midlothian*: 'the whole argued neglect and discomfort; the consequence, however, of idleness and indifference, not of poverty'.

Peffermill was to suffer even greater indignity in Victorian times when its sturdy Renaissance proportions were partitioned and many of its original walls and features concealed under plaster. A year after the Groves-Raines' took on the house, and after a great deal of labour and the removal of twenty-five skips containing the rejected accretions of the previous two centuries (mostly the building materials of Peffermill's 'Victorianisation') the house was transformed into an ideal family home with architects' offices at ground level where the original vestibule welcomed Edward Edgar's seventeenth-century visitors of the 'middling sort'.

The National Trust for Scotland has been a consistent restorer of Renaissance buildings. It acquired Craigievar, the jewel of the north-east, in 1963 and during re-harling ten years later evidence was uncovered to suggest that the hall assumed its present form between 1610 and 1626 when the castle was owned by William Forbes of Menie, nicknamed 'Danzig Willie' as a result of the fortune he made from trade in the Baltic. The oak panelling in the room is the work of local craftsmen, probably of the Aberdeen school, and contemporary with the ceiling.

Craigievar is a superb example of the ability of what was called 'the middling sort' (the lairds, new feuars and the rising professions) to create towerhouse symbols of the new leisured class which often matched or outshone the homes of the nobility. The seventeenth century produced a literary intelligentsia too, largely made up of the professions and lairds. Architecture was an up-and-coming profession. Towards the end of the seventeenth century Sir William Bruce (*c.*1630–1710), 'the introducer of Architecture into this country' espoused the classical formal house style, modestly at first in his recasting of Tweeddale House in 1664, on a larger scale at Balcaskie in 1668–74, and gloriously in Kinross House and Hopetoun House. 'Bruce's position and earlier political career (Jacobite though he was) made him the social equal of those gentlemen-amateurs who enjoyed architecture as an intellectual pursuit, collecting books on the subject for their libraries and sharing an enthusiasm for antiquity in general and the historical origins of classical architecture in particular,' observes Margaret Sanderson in

Robert Adam and Scotland. The Renaissance buildings of the sixteenth and seventeenth centuries, built in the native tradition, displayed European influences, but now gentleman-amateur and professional architects alike followed Sir William Bruce's lead in looking to England for inspiration and touring its country houses. John, 6th Earl of Mar (1675–1732) was an outstanding contemporary gentleman-architect whose schemes, like Bruce's, included landscaping as well as architecture. Many educated Scots had emigrated, in the wake of the religious reforms of John Knox (whose condemnation of the unreformed countries of Europe unwittingly nudged Scotland closer to England), and on the trail blazed by James VI and I (who swept up the court to London and took fourteen years to come back for a visit), emboldened by the international perspective of scholars, artists, merchants and soldiers who went before them. Colen Campbell (1676–1729) and James Gibbs (1682–1754) two of the most influential Scottish architects who settled and practised in London, were followed by the finest architect of the next generation, Robert Adam, and his brother John. Campbell published his influential *Vitruvius Britannicus,* promoting the architectural style of Andrea Palladio, the sixteenth-century Italian maestro, and James Gibbs became surveyor of the fabric of Wren's London churches, writing several books which expanded the reference library available to the eighteenth-century architect. Both men were European in outlook and influenced the development of the profession in Scotland where, by the 1720s, classical architecture flourished and where the practice of William Adam, steeped in the tradition of craftsmen-architects, nevertheless synthesised the universal influences of his age. As the seventeenth century wore on the 'good and greit' no longer aspired to live in towerhouses, but in temples.

In an age of relative prosperity privileged lairds and merchants enjoyed what were effectively the first country houses. Home became a delightful retreat where vivid ceilings, like the Celestial Ceiling at Cullen depicting Flora and Mars, married heaven to earth in a glorious painted cacophony of motifs inspired by the galaxy and the natural world, mythology and biblical stories. Like the broch and the towerhouse, the painted ceiling is a Scottish phenomenon rarely found in England. The painted ceiling above all other Renaissance artifacts symbolises Scotland's lost golden age. The Cullen ceiling was destroyed by fire in the late 1980s.

The 'hie burde' or long feasting table has gone from the Great Hall at Doune Castle but it is still possible to imagine this splendid chamber as the scene of 'large tabling and bellycheer' in its day. The open-timber roof, minstrels' gallery and central fire-basket are Victorian additions.

Timber furnishings and brightly painted ceiling joists at Newark Castle remain intact from 1599: the door to the right leads to the privy or toilet-closet; the wall panelling contains a cupboard and the wall recess on the left once contained a press-bed, or folding bed.

The cabinet, or small room off the Queen's Chamber within the royal lodging at Edinburgh Castle where the future King James VI of Scotland and I of England was born to Mary, Queen of Scots, on 19 June 1566. The ceiling and upper panelling date from the period of refurbishment between 1615 and 1617 which anticipated the ageing monarch's return to his birthplace. The wall painting of the Royal Arms of Scotland, 1617, is by John Anderson.

The 1578 Sheffield Portrait of Mary, Queen of Scots, shows a 'small pattern Holbein carpet'.

James VI *c.*1579–80.
Woodcut from Beza's *Icones* attributed to
Adrian Vanson.

John Knox *c.*1579–80.
Woodcut from Beza's *Icones* attributed to
Adrian Vanson.

James Stewart, 1st of Traquair, received a grant of the property in 1492 and it is likely that he built a small, free-standing towerhouse of three storeys with an attic which is referred to as the 'turris et fortalicium de Trakware' in a charter granted to his son William in 1512. A south wing, with stair tower rising to the height of the original tower, was added in the middle of the 16th century and another wing to the south later with a window-lintel on the west front inscribed with the initials of Sir William Stewart, 5th of Traquair, 1599. This laird also remodelled the southern end of the house and rebuilt the kitchen wing. Further alterations continued throughout the 17th century and when Traquair was the home of John, 1st Earl of Traquair, who became Lord High Treasurer of Scotland in 1636, it was referred to as the 'Palace' of Traquair. Plans for remodelling the main block with a new forecourt and service wings were drawn up in 1695. Instead of the remodelling, a series of minor alterations was made, including the insertion of new windows and lavish redecoration of the principal apartments including new panelling. The new forecourt and service wings were constructed after 1695. Again, in the middle of the 18th century, plans were drawn up for the remodelling of the main block. An unsigned sheet of drawings shows a scheme with a classical façade, but fortunately these schemes got no further than the drawing-board and Traquair remained largely itself, apart from internal remodelling of the service wings, the conversion of part of the ground floor of the south wing into living accommodation, and later, the construction of a new stable and brewhouse, a chapel and extensive internal refurbishment.

Traquair House: early 17th-century door depicting *fleur de lis* spandrils and a unicorn goring a lion, both standing on the back of an elephant and howdah.

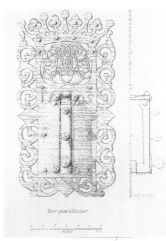

Door-plate & Knocker

Traquair House: main entrance door, wrought-iron knocker plate, decorated with an earl's coronet, an intricate reversed monogram CSETMM for Charles Stewart, 4th Earl of Traquair and his wife Mary Maxwell with the date 1705.

The rare oak-panelled ceiling of the Long Gallery at Crathes is made of finely cut panels overlaid with a pattern of moulded ribs in diamond and oblong formations. The ribs are punctuated by coats of arms and recurrent motifs of the holly leaf emblem of the founding Burnett family and the Horn of Leys. The centre rib displays six shields belonging to the first baronet, the King of Scotland, (his overlord), the Marquis of Hamilton, (his cousin), Lord Dunfermline, the Chancellor of Scotland and a close friend, Alexander Burnett, his great-grandfather and Gilbert Burnett, Bishop of Salisbury. The remaining woodwork is 19th century. Like Craigievar, Crathes was a product

of local stonemaking and carving skills. It is likely that the remarkable family of master masons called Bell, who worked in the Aberdeen area, also built Midmar and Castle Fraser. The Horn of Leys (which hangs over the Hall fireplace) is said to have been given to the first Burnett of Leys by Robert the Bruce in 1323 as a symbol of his authority as a Royal Forester. Burnett was an Anglo-Saxon who moved to the Scottish Borders with Norman English families and later settled in the north east. His descendant Alexander Burnett married Janet Hamilton in 1543 and founded Crathes. Meetings of the laird's court were sometimes held in the Long Gallery instead of the Hall and the

photograph shows 17th century chairs and oak tables laid out for this occasion. The floral marquetry cabinet is English c.1685.

The Hall at Craigievar: its soaring vaulted ceiling, massive fireplace with elaborate overmantel plasterwork, screens and musicians' gallery gloriously marry traditional forms with Renaissance expression. Although its profusion of gables and turrets inspired many 19th-century architects, Craigievar escaped 'Victorianisation' and the exterior remains very much as it was in 1626 when it was completed. The National Trust acquired Craigievar in 1963 and, while re-harling the castle ten years later, it uncovered evidence to suggest that the Hall assumed its present form between 1610 and 1626 when the castle was owned by William Forbes of Menie. Forbes was nicknamed 'Danzig Willie' as a result of the fortune he made from trade in the Baltic. The splendid decoration of the Hall was the work of journeyman plasterers who travelled widely and worked in Scotland and England in the early 17th century. The moulds used at Craigievar were also used at Bromley-by-Bow in 1606, Glamis in 1620 and Muchalls in 1624. The plasterwork above the massive granite lintel of the fireplace is one of the most magnificent examples of British heraldry in this form. The arms of William Forbes and his wife Margaret Woodward appear on either side of the central pendant. As tenant-in-chief of the Crown, the laird of Craigievar was entitled to display his achievement and his authority to administer justice over his lands in the King's name at barony courts. The oak panelling in the room is the work of local craftsmen, probably of the Aberdeen school, and contemporary with the ceiling. The 17th-century oak dining table, like other furniture found in the castles and country houses of the north-east, originated from the Low Countries. The armchairs are covered in Forbes tartan woven in the 19th century and the carpet was made to match in 1970.

Traquair House: part of an embroidered panel showing fruits, flowers, animals and birds. This panel is one of several discovered recently, carefully stored away in trunks at Traquair House, uncut, unused and revealing the brilliant colours of decorative hangings in the late 16th and early 17th century.

George Jamesone: self-portrait in a room hung with pictures c.1637–40

One of the earliest paintings to show interior details: *Anne Erskine, Countess of Rothes with her Daughters* (1626) portrayed by George Jamesone.

Northfield House: typical naturalistic
motifs painted on the beam-and-
board ceiling discovered in the 1950s
under a later plaster ceiling which
helped to conserve the original
vibrancy of the work.

The fine painted ceiling in the first Lord's Hall at Huntingtower Castle is regarded as the earliest surviving tempera-painted ceiling.

Two sections of the 1620 Strathmore Carpet, a reproduction Turkey-work carpet, hand-knotted and piled with jute warp and weft, and made in Norwich, England.

A valance from a bed formerly at Balloch (Taymouth Castle), now in the Burrell Collection, shows scenes of Adam and Eve in Paradise and their expulsion from the Garden. The Campbell and Ruthven arms of the owners are surmounted by their initials and a true lovers' knot suspended from a ram's head.

This splendid 1594 carved oak bed made for Alexander Burnett, great-grandson of the founder of Crathes, and his wife Katherine is decorated with holly leaves, boars' heads and the Horn of Leys. Fine carving like this is associated with the Aberdeen school of wood carving.

Hans Memling (*c.*1430–94) showed the Virgin's bed hung with red curtains, one looped up, with a narrow flat pelmet hiding the curtain rods, in this painting of the *Annunciation*, now in the Burrell Collection, Glasgow.

Gladstane's Land, a six-storey tenement with arcade at street level, was built in 1600 and bought by Thomas Gledstanes, a merchant, in 1617. By 1635 he had sold off most of the tenement and lived on the top floor, far away from the stench of the street. The bed in the chamber is hung with fabric embroidered with crewel work, a typical 17th century domestic hanging which emulated brightly painted bedcover panels imported from India.

For five centuries the lands of Towie were held by the Barclays whose ancestor, John de Berkeley, is thought to bave been an Anglo-Norman Knight who accompanied Queen Margaret to Scotland on her marriage to Malcolm III and was granted estates in the northern kingdom. According to a 16th century stone, one of his sons, Sir Alexander Barclay, was the first of the Barclays who inherited Towie. Another stone records that his descendant, Sir Walter Barclay, 'foundet' the castle in 1210. A later Sir Walter received a Crown charter of the lands of 'Tolly' from Robert the Bruce. Succeeding generations of Barclays intermarried with leading Aberdeenshire families including the Inneses, Gordons, Hays and Forbeses. The male line of the Barclays ended in 1668 with the death of Patrick Barclay whose estates passed to his daughter Elizabeth, wife of John Gordon of Rothiemay. In 1752 Towie Barclay was sold to the Earl of Findlater and two centuries of neglect began, until 1969 when Marc and Karen Ellington purchased and restored the castle, adding a caphouse within the Victorian parapet.

The Ellingtons decided to furnish the Laird's Hall at Towie Barclay to emphasise its original baronial status and Gothic character rather than attempt to reproduce an authentic 'period' room. 17th century Scottish chairs do, however, join with a solid Dutch table and oak serving table, a carved cupboard displays pewter ware authentically enough, and a Turkey-style rug covers the table. Other rugs have slipped to the floor, as they tended to do from the 18th century. Out of the picture, the huge fireplace forms an inglenook with narrow stone benches along its sides. The upper part of the Hall's south wall opens through a broad arch into an oratory on whose ceiling the heraldic scheme reaches its culmination and includes the arms of Christ himself. As John Gifford comments: 'Sir Patrick Barclay was a Roman Catholic who had signed the Band for Defence of the True Religion against Protestantism in 1589. In the oratory he could hear Mass, perhaps with his servants watching from the hall below'.

Kinross House, which he built for himself, and Hopetoun House, which William Adam later remodelled, are regarded as Sir William Bruce's finest houses. This plan drawing of Kinross House and gardens is attributed to Alexander Edward.

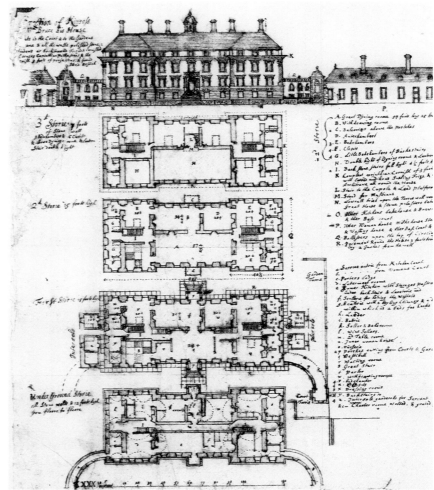

The towerhouses of the north-east, sometimes referred to as 'castle country', have a timeless and poetic beauty and even in a country and a county famed for towerhouses, Craigievar stands out as the foremost example of the baronial style which was, and still is, Scotland's finest contribution to European domestic architecture. Its profusion of gables and turrets inspired many 19th century architects but Craigievar escaped 'Victorianisation' and remians very much as it was in 1626, the year of its completion.

The family coat of arms of Edward Edgar and Margaret Pearson who built Peffermill House in 1636 is inscribed above the entrance. Sir John Gilmour purchased the house in 1661 to add to the Craigmillar Castle estate and the property stayed in the hands of the Gilmour of Liberton family trust until 1982 when architects Nicholas and Limma Groves-Raines acquired it from the local authority in a derelict condition. They converted the house to contain architectural offices in the old ground level cellars, accommodation for the family and a caretakers' flat on the second floor: 'A more authentic restoration would have transformed Peffermill into one house with the kitchen on the ground floor to make use of the original fireplace and a back door out to the formal herb and rose garden we have recreated,' says Limma Groves-Raines. Like other Renaissance homes, Peffermill was 'Victorianised' in the 19th century and the cost of stripping back raised doors and windows, small fireplaces, cornices and plaster ceilings would have been prohibitive. This late 20th century restoration, then, was a working compromise which balanced historical authenticity with economic realities. The house changed hands in 1995.

The atmosphere of this corner of Peffermill's Hall suggests a Dutch Renaissance painting. 20th century decorative additions include the off-white painted floor. The unpainted beam-and-board ceiling is likely to have been painted in the 17th century. The architects who restored the house found painted wall decoration at one end of the hall. The Victorian sash windows were left: a compromise between authenticity and economic reality. Increased light is, in any case, valued by 20th century residents. Although the Paisley Shawl is Victorian, its pattern and colour, and that of the rugs, pay due regard to the colourful Renaissance interiors which originally graced Peffermill.

The original turnpike stair leads to what the Groves-Raines' might describe as a 'semi-authentic' Hall, a delightful family living room, whose dimensions have been restored and the accretions of two centuries stripped away to reveal bare simplicity. New pine doors are punctuated with copies of 17th century handmade nails and missing stone corbels replaced and 'aged' with a needle gun. The result is a Hall which emulates the freshness and lightness of Renaissance interiors in stripped pine floors, biscuit-coloured ceiling, door and half-shutter wood, painted plaster walls and appropriate furniture.

CLASSICAL STYLE
1700–1830

'Scotland is But a narrow place,

besides whoever he go's partner with can play their Cards better

with a London partner than without'

James Smith's (*c.* 1645–1731) estate of Whitehill, later renamed Newhailes, became a seat of Scottish Enlightenment.

Scotland entered the new century an unwilling bride. Tradition has it that the bells of St Giles rang the folk tune : *How can I be sad on my wedding day?* It was the 1st of May 1707 and the bride on that day of Union felt neither Scots nor British.

The series of shocks that sounded down the last decades of the seventeenth century had been fired by Reformation zeal and Jacobitism rather than cultural animation. The Glorious Revolution of 1688–9 had put William and Mary on the English throne and re-established Presbyterianism. Although Lowland Scotland affected little love for the Highland tribes, its population was nevertheless shocked by the king's connivance in the murder of the MacDonalds of Glencoe in 1692, an atrocity signed for by the hand of John Dalrymple, Master of Stair. Two years earlier the same Lord Advocate had ordered the worse slaughter of Clanranald on Eigg: 'the only popish clan in the kingdom and it will be popular to take severe course with them'. The Jacobite, Graham of Claverhouse, had lost his life at Killiecrankie in 1689 and religious schisms rumbled on. But even these events were overshadowed by the betrayal of Scots settlers in the Darien Peninsula and the heavy loss of investment in the scheme to establish a Scots trading colony there in 1698. The Alien Act which followed in 1705 further fuelled Scots outrage: it effectively prevented trading between Scotland and England and stated that, henceforth, Scots would be regarded as aliens in England (but not, of course, the other way round). Against a background of unrest and violence in the capital, the Articles of Union were prepared by the Scottish Parliament. The anguish of the shotgun bride set her descendants' teeth on edge for several generations as, quite literally, Scots became ashamed to use their native tongue.

Allan Ramsay, a founder member of the Easy Club 'for mutual improvement in Conversation' in 1712, later opened a bookshop under his own 'Union' signboard representing the poet William Drummond (1585–1649) and Ben Jonson the English dramatist who had visited Drummond at Hawthornden near Roslin in 1618. Writers and poets wanted to express themselves in English as well as in Scots and intellectuals, including David Hume and Adam Ferguson, felt the need to anglicize their speech, particularly on visits to London. As trade, cultural and political links opened up, elocution lessons became the vogue among the established as well as the aspiring.

The Jacobite issue split the country, too. The professional and merchant classes in Edinburgh understood the romance of the Pretender's cause but supported the government. It was the established women of the city, wearing breast-knots and favours, who entertained Charles Edward Stuart at their private assemblies. When the prince rode out of Traquair House in 1745, the family closed the Bear Gates and they have never been opened since. Allan Ramsay dodged the Jacobite issue when the Pretender was in Edinburgh by taking refuge in Penicuik House. Sir James Clerk rebuilt the house he inherited from his father, Sir John, who played a formative role in the evolution of classical architecture. Indeed, Penicuik House, 'set in a romantic, yet classically inspired landscape', was considered one of the marvels of the day.

It was Sir John Clerk of Penicuik (1676–1755), doyen of the gentlemen-amateurs, who called William Bruce 'the introducer of Architecture into this country'. Sir William, who became Overseer of the Royal Works in Scotland, was succeeded by a contemporary who, in the course of a long life, straddled the late Renaissance and early classical periods. James Smith (c.1645–1731) was described as an 'architectour, a man who has the repute to be very skilled in works of that nature', and as 'the most experienced architect in Scotland'. Smith married a daughter of Robert Mylne (1633–1710), who had been a master mason to the crown and profited from speculative building, including Edinburgh's Milne's Court and Milne's Square, and Smith worked with Bruce as a master mason in the restoration of the Palace of Holyroodhouse in 1678. He was a classical architect designing an impressive list of country houses for the growing class of nouveau gentry, which included the craftsmen-architects to which Smith himself belonged, as well as for the Dukes of Hamilton and Queensberry, the Duchess of Buccleuch and other nobility.

Scots architectural style now filtered through England and the style in vogue was early Palladian, which in Scotland was straightforward, and each new house was unique: internally the central hall gave access to from two to four apartments through one or more 'temple' porticos. Externally the lower storey was rusticated at ground or basement level below the ashlar upper storeys. Entry was through the 'rustic' or directly into the hall behind the portico, reached by an external flight of steps built out from the rustic with an additional rustic entrance, as at James Smith's own house near Musselburgh, this, however, being added here by a later builder. Smith's estate of Whitehill, renamed Newhailes, became the home of the Dalrymples and a seat of the Scottish Enlightenment which was led by the philosopher David Hume.

Roughly speaking, the first Newhailes, which housed James Smith's ten children, is the central core of the present house. Sir David Dalrymple bought it in 1707 and within ten years what had been an old-fashioned house was becoming something considerably grander, with a procession of rooms including a State

Apartment and Library wing. But the true 'builder of Newhailes' is regarded as Sir James Dalrymple who altered the entrance from north to south and carried forward his father's intentions to create an enlarged baroque house which was complete by 1757, although its exterior escaped a baroque façade. The spirit of Sir James presides from a vivid portrait overlooking the dining room where the Thomas Clayton plasterwork, the William Strachan carved woodwork, the marble chimneypiece ordered by Sir James from the workshops of the Cheere brothers in London, the olive green painterwork and gilding, the woodcarving on doors, shutters and dados have been preserved since the 1730s. The rococo decoration includes plasterwork festoons, garlands of fruits and flowers, egg-and-dart and key pattern carvings, lion heads, eagles and scallop shells. Perhaps it was the house's proximity to the sea that inspired the exquisite set of gilded door furniture, works of fine craftsmanship, depicting fronds of seaweed in which a cockle shell has been captured to hide the door key. Gilded seashells are a recurring motif throughout the house, in the form of real shells gathered from the shore less than a mile away, or replicas in plaster or wood. Over the years some have inevitably fallen off but the present custodian collects them carefully in little piles, ready to be put back in place. The most gorgeous representation is in the library where two exaggerated scallop shells interclasp to crown the overmantel decoration. The scallop shell, a medieval symbol of pilgrimage, particularly to Santiago de Compostella in northern Spain, remained a potent decorative motif in the eighteenth century.

The Dalrymples of Newhailes were singularly favoured in the eighteenth century. Frequent trips to London and the south kept them in touch with cultural, social and political developments. The head of the family from the 1750s was the great grandson of the 1st Viscount Stair, the cryptic Law Lord, Lord Hailes, who played a leading role in the imaginative and intellectual development of the Scottish Enlightenment. Historian, legal writer, translator and man of letters, Lord Hailes's correspondence, literary and historical manuscripts, legal and estate papers form the only extant complete archive of a man of his stature in eighteenth-century Scotland. At a desk piled high with research volumes in the Library wing Lord Hailes wrote the original manuscript of the *Annals of Scotland* which was annotated by no less a person than Dr Johnson. And in this room, which must often have provided a meeting place for the great figures of the Scottish Enlightenment, James Boswell first resolved to meet Dr Johnson who had so impressed Lord Hailes in London. The valuable Newhailes collection of library and archive was removed for safekeeping to the National Library of Scotland in 1976.

In the first decades of the eighteenth century, James Smith's architectural practice disappeared off the scene and William Adam's flourished on the back of an unprecedented building boom promoted by Union supporters who required palaces to match the self-esteem bestowed by their new titles and wealth. Jacobites, who aspired to jump on the bandwagon by becoming clients of Adam's practice, did not, however, have the money to get their buildings constructed. Sir John Clerk was an outstanding Scots example of the eighteenth-century dilettanti: someone who took delight in all the arts. Influential London wits like Lord Burlington were included in his circle, the Academia dell'Arcadia, which attracted cultured Scots like William Adam and Allan Ramsay and his painter son to his home in Midlothian. In his role as Baron of Exchequer, Clerk had described William Adam to a meeting of the treasury as 'a person of approved Skill and Integrity in Architecture' and after Clerk recommended him to survey the roof at Holyrood, William Adam attracted lucrative contracts including works at Fort George and developments for an influential group of noblemen and landowners including the Duke of Hamilton, the Earls of Stair and Hopetoun, the Marquess of Tweeddale and Lord Marchmont. To the latter, Adam recommended the use of stucco: 'it is a Plaister much us'd now in Publick rooms, such as the Hall, Dining Room, Parlour, etc. etc. And my Lord Burlington has done the floors of some of his room with it in imitation of Marble. It can be made of any Colour, or vein'd as marble - it does Not suffer by washing, but rather [it] hardens . . .'

But even as William Adam embraced the classical manner, he looked over his shoulder to the architects of the Renaissance, and to the baroque buildings he had seen for himself in Holland and France. The 'full-blooded grandeur' of the baroque, comments Ian Gow 'displayed all the ornaments known to architecture' and expressed the pretensions of Adam's post-Union clients. He collected antique books on architecture for his library as well as the works of James Gibbs and Sir John Vanbrugh, and Colen Campbell's *Vitruvius Britannicus,* which promoted Palladianism and inspired William Adam's *Vitruvius Scoticus* (published posthumously in 1812) which advertised his own talents. The exteriors of William Adam's houses are imbued with individualistic character, as at Dun and Arniston. And he indulged his love of dramatic effect and surface decoration within the restraints he set himself in his interiors, such as the drawing room at House of Dun. His interior plans supplied 'a following of rooms: a great dining room, a drawing room, a bedchamber and a closet with an optional hall and great staircase to extend the processional route through a house'. The largest room was the great dining room, which tended to make his plans asymmetrical. It was an arrangement which had been fashionable in the south over twenty years before and it is possible that this archaic form lingered longer in the north. Like many contemporaries of his own 'polite society', including Sir John Clerk, William Adam set out on tours of English country houses, which were often remote and isolated with difficult access. Grand houses and grounds were open to visitors to view rather like the network of historic houses open to the public today. Then, as now, many of these 'powerhouses', to quote Mark Girouard's term, were marvels of the day.

William Adam took the lead in the Scottish building boom, aided by his sons James, John and Robert. Robert Adam in particular gave the family name to the celebrated style that was to become the hallmark of good taste from Moscow to Monticello. While the father's interior decorations struck a note of architectural grandeur previously unknown in Scotland, his brilliant son Robert would go on to make what Ian Gow refers to as 'England's bleak and symmetrical Palladian palaces' more sumptuously comfortable for their second generation of occupants. By the time of William Adam's death in 1748, Scottish and English taste had begun to converge and the Scottish baroque waned. London architects made neo-classical designs for Scottish houses such as Isaac Ware's Amisfield and, later, William Chambers designed Duddingston House and the Dundas Mansion in St Andrew Square. Some of Chippendale's finest rococo mahogany furniture was dispatched brand new to Scottish patrons. If a Scottish practice could be run from London there was little to keep ambitious young designers like Robert Adam at home.

Robert Adam left Scotland for Italy in 1754, only in some ways typical of the 'troops of well-born young men' who set out on the grand tour every year. 'They flocked round picture galleries, they congregated in the ruins of Rome, they directed excavations, and they bought Greek and Roman statues – often faked – and old masters of doubtful authenticity,' comments Mark Girouard. And they commissioned portraits from artists, including Pompeo Batoni who in 1766 depicted William Gordon of Fyvie in modified Highland dress, victoriously posturing beside a statue of Roma. Robert was well born in the sense that his family was close knit. His father was already an outstanding architect, and the Adam family was well off. They operated between the craftsmen-architect-building-trade world of 'mechanick things' and the 'polite society' of their patrons. Although Robert, the aspiring young architect, joined the ranks of the tourist dilettanti, he also invested a great deal of his capital in studying and drawing. He was accompanied to Italy by the Hon. Charles Hope, brother of Lord Hopetoun.

Established families now had to find space for the collections the 'new dilettanti' brought home from the grand tour as well as for the accumulations of their ancestors. The answer was to build larger houses or enlarge existing ones, as Sir James Clerk did at Penicuik House. Robert Adam, splendidly established in his London practice by 1770, extended Newby Hall in Yorkshire to display the collection of Greek and Roman sculpture of its owner. Greek and Roman civilization continued to be considered the basis of modern civilization and the idea of the classical orders informed architecture. Until the Gothic was espoused by Robert Adam and others, the Platonists of the eighteenth century pursued perfection in their homes, their landscaped gardens and in themselves, to fit them as members of the ruling classes.

In Scotland, though, ultimate perfection was tempered by the sense that the axis of the world turned elsewhere. The idea of 'London' became both a curse and a blessing to eighteenth-century Scots and remains so today: 'Scotland is But a narrow place, besides whoever he go's partner with can play their Cards better with a London partner than without,' James Adam had written to Robert, concerning the possibility of their brother William joining him in London. In London and the great homes of the south, Robert Adam had set out to become the most fashionable architect of all, working in town and country for patrons including London Scots: Lord Mansefield's Kenwood House, the Earl of Bute's Luton Park, Sir Lawrence Dundas's Moor Park and London houses of the Earls of Fife and Eglinton. Other architects with Scottish connections included William Chambers, Robert's nearest rival, who was one of the first to do away with the rustic, opening up the rooms of his Duddingston House directly to gardens and greenery. Both men kept lively contact with Scotland but their life's work was English-based. The taste of aristocratic clients was firmly identified now with metropolitan fashion and the developing middle-class market could be satisfied by Scottish architects and craftsmen.

Scotland, and particularly a poverty-stricken Scotland whose independence had perished in 1707, might seem an unlikely seedbed for the propagation of the decorative arts among 'the middling sort'. Yet the first dawning of awareness of good contemporary interior design in homes can be traced to this period, through William Adam and his sons, to the Board of Trustees for Manufactures set up in 1727 to encourage economic development by stimulating industry, and particularly the domestic textile industries of the infant Scottish economy, thus hoping to relieve Scotland's all-pervasive poverty. Ian Gow describes the Board, which founded an innovatory school in Edinburgh in 1760 to train young designers, as combining something of the modern functions of Scottish Enterprise and the Arts Council to which the guilty conscience of a post-Union parliament had voted a substantial 'slush fund'. The Board, eager to elevate humble domestic textiles like linen and carpets which played an important part in the Scottish economy, encouraged high standards of design. None of the students' designs survive, although an outstanding carpet design submitted by the young Alexander Nasmyth to gain admission to the Board's school is in the collection of the National Galleries of Scotland. Understated neo-classical designs like this and other designs associated with David Allan, a Master of the Academy, reveal the excellent standard of draughtsmanship apprentice tradesmen received at the school.

Everybody who was anybody aspired to go on the grand tour, whose focus was Italy, but Scots increasingly toured England and vice versa. Visitors, drawn by the pictureque landscape, found Scotland to be 'a country almost as little known to its southern brethren as Kamschatska' according to Thomas Pennant who undertook his first tour of Scotland in 1769. Martin Martin's seventeenth-century account of the Western Isles probably inspired both Pennant and Dr Johnson to tour Scotland. Daniel Defoe had his own political reasons for visiting Scotland before his *Tour of the Whole Island of Great Britain* put Scotland on the map once more, and later in the century the *terra incognita* was part of the indigenous tourist trail engaged by cultivated ladies and gentlemen. *Ars Peregrinandi* was part of civilized life and to visit the great homes of Scotland was to elevate the art. Pennant visited Bruce's houses Kinross and Hopetoun: 'the handsomest I saw in North Britain'. He took in the grand houses of the day noting little more than the contents of their picture galleries in his *Tour of Scotland*, notably the one at Hamilton Palace: 'of great extent and furnished (as well as some other rooms) with excellent paintings'. Blair Atholl 'was once fortified and held a siege against the Rebels in 1746; but at present is much reduced in height, and the inside highly finished by the noble owner. The most singular piece of furniture is a chest of drawers made of broom, most elegantly striped in veins of white and brown.' He found areas of thriving industry in the Highlands: 'owing to the abolition of the feudal tenures, or vassalage; for before that was effected . . . the Strong oppressed the Weak, the Rich the Poor'; but in Inveraray and other areas he found 'the most wretched hovels that can be imagined'. At Lochaber he found people living in structures framed with upright wattle poles, the roofs 'formed of boughs like a wigwam, and the whole is covered with sods; so that in this moist climate their cottages have a perpetual and much finer verdure than the rest of the country'. It would be a long time before the working poor had houses, let alone interiors, of any note.

Attempts to deal with the overcrowding in the Old Town of Edinburgh by providing good accommodation for the better-off had been made in the sixteenth century by the development of garden ground and in the seventeenth century by the construction of monumental tenements in the Lawnmarket: Robertson's Close, Milne's Court and Milne's Square. High tenements continued to be built in the eighteenth century: James Court in 1723 and the front block of Advocates' Close about 1735. But these developments had done nothing much to relieve the problem: 'for though many Cities have more people in them, yet, I believe, this may be said with Truth,' wrote Daniel Defoe, 'that in no City in the World so many People live in so little Room as at *Edinburgh*'.

Daniel Defoe was sent to Edinburgh to report to the government on Scottish attitudes to the Act of Union and on trade potential. In 1710 he edited the *Edinburgh Courant* from Moubray House, which must have changed little since the Renaissance, apart from the addition of panelling and a fine plasterwork ceiling in the second floor room of the lower house. A shrewd observer of life in the Old Town, Defoe later wrote: 'The City suffers infinite Disadvantages, and lies under such scandalous

Inconveniences as are, by its Enemies, made a Subject of Scorn and Reproach; as if the People were not as willing to live sweet and clean as other nations, but delighted in Stench and Nastiness: whereas, were any other People to live under the same Unhappiness, I mean as well of a rocky and mountainous Situation, throng'd Buildings, from seven to ten or twelve story high, a Scarcity of Water, and that little they have difficult to be had, and to the uppermost Lodgings, far to fetch; we should find a London, or a Bristol as dirty as Edinburgh, and, perhaps, less able to make their Dwelling tolerable, at least in so narrow a Compass.'

Knowledge of London life intensified the cry of the better-off in Edinburgh that they could no longer live in the filth, squalor and overcrowding of the Old Town. The developments in the Old Town had brought relief to a few privileged citizens but many more 'superior' people – judges, advocates, writers and clerks, bankers, merchants and tradesmen – began to clamour for better accommodation too. The Act of Union may have deprived Scotland of its own parliament and Privy Council, but, as John Gifford reminds us, it was still a university town, the seat of the Scottish law courts, the base of an army in Edinburgh Castle with its own commander-in-chief, and a social and intellectual centre. The nobility and gentry desired to escape the tedium of winter in a country seat, where they risked being cut off by snow or muck for weeks on end, by residing in Edinburgh if they were not among the London émigrés. And it was increasingly important for the aspiring, too, to participate in Edinburgh parties and assemblies where suitable marriages might be made for their children.

The new tenements of the Royal Mile, most of which stand today, must have been expensive to build and, although they look uncompromisingly plain from the outside, their interiors were large and often lavish. John Gifford, writes revealingly of some: 'In 1742 the merchant and MP, Alexander Stuart, occupied a nine roomed flat in James Court, three with marble chimneypieces, one further dignified by a mirror overmantel. Rooms were usually panelled, the woodwork sometimes forming a frame for tapestry. Painting of the pine panelling could display a variety of effects. The unambitious might opt for an overall green colour scheme but each Edinburgh painter at the end of his apprenticeship was required to demonstrate his skill in graining and marbling.'

John Gifford has examined surviving specifications which show that the interior decoration of these flatted houses was often elaborate: 'In 1757 Alexander Weir was required to paint a room of a Mr Sheill's flat as follows: 'in fine white primed in oil and finished in Varnish, with a piece of ornament on the chimney-piece pannel & over the four door-heads and to enrich the ovalls round the Door egg & dart and paint the chimney stone dove colour marble.' In this decorative scheme paint effects were used in place of costly marble and intricately carved detail. But the following year John Dallas was requested to execute an even more ambitious decorative scheme in

Robert Farquhar's flat where the plastered passage walls ended up looking like rusticated masonry, the wooden door architraves like pink marble and the pine doors like dark mahogany: 'to paint the Transe . . . Six foot high rustic stone work in oil with an Astragal moulding round the top, the outsides of the Doors Mohogony, the Architraves round ye doors Flushed marble . . . also to take the dimensions of the Chimney-piece in the Dining roum and paint a landskip for it. To gild the moulding round the said Landskip, To paint festoons on the heads of the three doors in the said dining roum and To make a niche at the East end of the Transe.'

John Clark decorated the front room of a flat rented by Robert Miller, a wright, also in 1758, to this specification: 'the body or walls of the roum silver grey primed and finished in Oile, The doors Mahogany colour, the Architraves of the Doors Dovecoloured marble, the Chimney stones Black marble, The foot of ye roum to be drawn about with chocolate colour and the roof to be white washed . . .'

Then as now, certain interior decorative fads were *de rigeur* in houses that were required to reflect the taste and social standing of their owners. These examples, and others of the period, show that marble-effect painterwork, mahogany door graining and *trompe l'oeil* effects were all the rage. 'Landskips', paintings of ruins set in landscapes, were ubiquitous adornments hung over mantelpieces and doors. More expensive stucco relief, of a military trophy as at the Chessel's Court flat, or of a cornucopia of flowers or a clamshell, provided an alternative to 'landskips' and houses and castles as grand as Newhailes and Culzean had both, the decorative paintings being executed by the Norie family.

Extravagant and modish though these tenement interiors were, they lurked in what Defoe described as 'Stench and Nastiness' without sanitation or adequate water supply. Drains built in the walls of new tenements were unsuccessful and stank incurably after a few years. Another writer in the 1730s lamented the malodorous habit of 'gardy loo': 'throwing over the windows all manner of Filth foull Water, ashes & ca', so that visitors thought, 'It Rains Dung from the Clouds every night'.

In the 1750s John Adam reported that Tweeddale House had fallen into serious disrepair and reconstructed it with his brother Robert, as well as building a fine residence for the judge and politician Lord Milton in the Canongate. The Canongate outwith the city walls (it was not formally incorporated into the City until 1856) offered some space for homes in which the rich could escape the garbage and noise of tenement life. Houses like this were set back from the street behind a court and with back gardens. Like the tenements of the Old Town, the exterior looked severe, but the interior of Milton House was graced with mural landscapes set in Watteauesque flower borders by William Delacour, and gilded cornices and ceilings embellished with stucco work. Delacour, a proficient artist in the French manner, was the school of the Board of Manufactures' first teacher of pattern design and drawing. He co-operated on interior schemes with the Adam brothers but only at Yester House does his decoration survive intact.

The nine rooms of a house of John Grant, a Baron of the Court of Exchequer, near the Netherbow were, as John Gifford comments, 'all neatly finished and painted . . . or paper'd, some with Chinese paper; a marble chimney-piece from the ceiling in one, concaves and slabs in two other of the rooms, the drawing-room elegantly fitted up, painted, gilded and carved in the newest taste.' It is lamentable that few mid-eighteenth-century Edinburgh interiors, and similarly exuberant interiors in Glasgow, survive today.

Daniel Defoe had noted the development potential of the land north of Edinburgh long before plans for the first New Town were approved: 'the City might have been extended upon the Plain below, and fine beautiful Street would, no Doubt, have been built there; nay, I question much, whether in Time, the high Streets would not have been forsaken, and the city, as we might say, run all out of its Gates to the North.'

At last, in 1767, a New Town began to be laid out on the land that Defoe had remarked on, of regular streets, squares and crescents of terraced houses interspersed with a few tenements and enhanced with gardens. The New and Old Towns were connected by a great bridge across the valley between. All the tenements and many of the houses were built speculatively, and some were sold before their interiors were finished, a practice which allowed the buyer to choose different qualities of cornice and chimneypiece. Others were finished quite cheaply by the developer and then sold or rented out for a year or two until they had dried out. When these were finally sold the new owner sometimes replaced the builder's standard fittings with more expensive ones. In the second half of the century Edinburgh boasted the finest Georgian housing development in Europe, next to London and Bath, while the other Scottish cities promoted their own developments.

'The smartest houses were custom-built,' observes John Gifford: 'the client making sure that he acquired a building whose interior was worthy of his self-esteem and able to display his taste. Ceilings might be enriched with shallow Adamish ovals of husks tied with neat bows; wooden chimneypieces might be decorated with shells or thistles and roses or marble chimneypieces carved with scenes from classical mythology; walls (now plastered) covered with delicate plaster panel frames.'

A description of a house in St Andrew Square on its completion in 1778 conveys the rich decoration of one of the earliest New Town interiors: the dining room's plaster-panelled walls were painted green with the mouldings picked out in white and green; above the marble chimneypiece was a 'superb ornament'. The parlour behind was covered in 'mock India paper'. In the first floor drawing room, hung with India paper, were a 'rich Sicilian marble chimney-piece and ornamented frame, in the French taste'.

Today, Queen Street has become a through-road for traffic crossing town and many of its houses recreated as offices. But in 1795 the first floor of one contained, 'two large and two small drawing-rooms; two pieces of this apartment are fitted up in a show of decoration unequalled in this country, and exceeded in none; the superb doors and shutters are panelled with plate glass, and the styles enriched with gilding of various shades in a simple and classical taste'.

Simple and classical taste may have been hallmarks of Georgian interiors, but there was scope for occasional flashes of exuberant eccentricity. The setting for an 1815 party given by Grace Baillie in her 'curious apartments on the ground floor of an old-fashioned corner house in Queen Street' is described by Elizabeth Grant in *Memoirs of a Highland Lady*: 'All the doors were taken away, all the movables carried off, the walls were covered with evergreens, through the leaves of which peeped the light of coloured lamps festooned about with garlands of coarse paper flowers. Her passages, parlours, bedrooms, cupboards, were all adorned en suite, and in odd corners were various surprises intended for the amusement of the visitors; a cage of birds here, a stuffed figure in a bower, water trickling over mossy stones into an ivy-covered basin, a shepherdess in white muslin, with a wreath of roses and a crook, offering ices; a Highland laddie in a kilt presenting lemonade, a cupid with cake, a gypsy with fruit. It was very ridiculous, and yet the effect was pretty.'

Where previously they had operated in huddled Old Town apartments, the lives of better-off citizens now expanded within the theatre of their own spacious public rooms. Then, as now, fashion and entertainment were bywords for furnishing a Georgian New Town interior. Towards the end of the construction of the New Town, in Danube Street, for example, drawing room windows were constructed almost to the floor so that the rooms appeared light and spacious and the cast-iron balconies outside, massed with pot plants, seemed like miniature gardens. This fashion had been introduced as early as 1786, notes John Gifford, by the banker and connoisseur Sir William Forbes, although he made the mistake of ordering balconies in London which turned out to be the wrong size for his Edinburgh windows.

By 1820, too, it was fashionable to display, in Gifford's words 'cluttered magnificence'. The drawing room of Mrs Ainslie's house in Melville Street was filled with 'Chairs, Sofas, Couches, Easy Chairs', all of maple wood covered with 'the Finest Blue Silk Damask'. The same damask was used for the window curtains which hung from 'Cornices of Mapple Wood, richly Gilded'. Light was reflected by huge gilt-framed mirrors, one a 'Magnificent Pier Mirror with Pier Table of Verde Antique marble, the Main Plate about 83 by 51 inches with Mirror beneath Table'. Mrs Ainslie's back drawing room furniture was of mahogany covered in scarlet cloth which matched the curtain fabric. On the floor of both rooms was 'Finest patent Velvet

Carpet'. Oriental china and cases of stuffed tropical birds provided islands of patterned colour.

Most of Edinburgh's classical interiors are intact and lived in today. Their preservation and conservation is the aim of the New Town Conservation Committee which was set up in 1970. As John Gifford says: 'Decoration and furnishings have been changed by the new-Georgians (sometimes referred to as 'Astragals' by fellow Scots and as 'Young Athenians' by London Georgians) but the rooms continue to evoke the gay social whirl for which they were intended to be the setting'.

But who made the furniture for the houses and flats of Edinburgh's New Town and the grand country houses springing up all over the countryside? It was widely believed that the furniture came from London and that between 1760 and 1820 Edinburgh had no cabinet maker of any distinction. The late Francis Bamford, for one, was not convinced and set out on a 'gradual discovery of the personalities of the men who made the furniture I like'. Little is known about William Adam's furniture. As Ian Gow says: 'In an age which viewed interior decoration as a branch of architecture, and which would ruthlessly cut paintings 'to fit', furnishings took secondary place to swirling stucco ceilings overhead'. The furnishings for Adam's finest interiors might well have been imported from London, although the Edinburgh-made furniture with its lion-paw feet, supplied to Holyrood under his supervision in 1740, is remarkably handsome. Two recorded gilded 'eagle' tables which once accompanied the furniture have been lost but the Holyrood collection contains what Ian Gow calls a 'splendidly dotty contemporary asymmetrical eagle sidetable' which is in the same spirit as Adam's stuccowork.

Clues like the Edinburgh-made Holyrood furniture first perplexed Bamford almost fifty years ago and set him off on the trail that would lead to the publication of *A Dictionary of Edinburgh Furniture makers 1660–1840*. His initial detective work proved disappointing as enquiries in the city's museums and antique shops and among Edinburgh *cognoscenti* failed to turn up leads. A breakthrough came when he was working on the family papers at Paxton House, Berwickshire, in the 1950s. He came across the receipts and accounts for furniture supplied in 1814–15 to the library and picture gallery of that splendid Palladian house. Most of the furniture detailed in the accounts was still in Paxton House and the firm which made it was owned by William Trotter, the sole partner in what had previously been the firm of Young, Trotter and Hamilton whose premises stood on the site now occupied by the Balmoral Hotel (formerly the North British Hotel) at the east end of Princes Street.

Francis Bamford was not convinced that William Trotter could have achieved such high standards of production and so individual a style of design in the absence of a long tradition of fine furniture making. So, armed with the Paxton clue, he was able to identify another cabinetmaker, Francis Brodie, whose shop in the Lawnmarket was below a sign depicting 'Palladio's Head'. The shop sign signals Brodie's cultural outlook in contrast with those of less cultivated wrights and cabinet makers who had never heard of the great Italian architect and is reminiscent of Allan Ramsay's enlightened sign depicting Drummond and Jonson.

Shortly after he had established his own business, Francis Brodie gained the patronage of some of the leading families and within five years William Adam recommended him to the Duke of Hamilton, who ordered a suite of furniture for his apartments at Holyrood Palace. Bamford had solved another mystery and, thus encouraged, continued his research with the discovery that Francis Brodie's son William, the notorious Deacon Brodie, was a partner in the firm of Brodie and Son from 1767. Bamford speculates that when the Deacon quite literally dropped from the Edinburgh scene, representatives of the rival firm of Young and Trotter were among the throng watching Brodie's execution for his part in an armed robbery of the Excise House in 1788. Young and Trotter were well-known upholsterers whose ambitions to break into the furniture market had been thwarted by Francis and William Brodie.

Now there was no holding them back. In the months following Deacon Brodie's execution, Young and Trotter supplied Lord Mount Stuart with furniture for his house on the Isle of Bute and the Dundas family with furniture for Arniston House in Midlothian. The government appointed the firm to fit up the royal apartments at Holyrood. In the next two years Young and Trotter became the pre-eminent firm of cabinetmakers and held on to its reputation for nearly fifty years.

William Trotter was the sole proprietor of the firm in 1809 and arguably the most successful furniture maker Scotland has ever produced. Later he was distinguished as a master of the Merchant Company and Lord Provost of the City of Edinburgh. 'His genius', suggests Francis Bamford 'was knowing his customers and the houses they wished to furnish, he decided that he must leaven the fashionable elegance prevailing among the English designers of Regency furniture with some suggestion of Scottish dignity. There is, too, in all his furniture a calculated appeal to the trait in the Scottish character which likes to receive full value for money. His products achieved an air of refined solidity; the materials used were quite clearly of fine quality; he made occasional use of brass inlay to decorate his furniture and, unlike his English contemporaries, he seldom seems to have fitted brass feet on his tables, preferring boldly carved lions' paws. In fact his success was founded on his belief that he must provide what his customers wanted to possess.' People who wanted to be in Edinburgh only for the season often rented a house and furniture. Sir John Peter Grant of Rothiemurchus took a three-year lease on 8 Picardy Place in 1817, for example, and rented his furniture from William Trotter and Co.

When Francis Bamford began his detective work, the names of the great cabinetmakers had been forgotten. But, thanks to him, William Trotter's name is on the lips of everyone interested in Georgian furniture again, as is the litany of significant furniture makers from 1660 to 1840 recorded in his dictionary.

By the 1770s, James and Robert Adam had established a substantial Scottish practice: one-third of its clients were Scots who might choose between classical style and castle style. Whatever the influences were that encouraged Robert Adam to develop these 'original creations of 18th century European architecture', his Scots clients who included Baillie of Mellerstain, Mure of Caldwell and Cassillis of Culzean, associated them with heredity and lost identity. 'The decoration of the interiors, however,' says Margaret Sanderson, 'especially the ceilings, is as sophisticated as that of any classical Adam house. The library [at Mellerstain], which has been described as having 'the effect of perfection', can be compared in quality with that at Osterley. The gallery at the top of the house, on the other hand, with its vaulted ceiling, is a feature found in many Scottish castles and may be seen at Craigievar.' And, at Culzean, the 10th Earl of Cassillis invited Robert Adam to indulge 'his romantic imagination'.

Later, in Edinburgh and the other cities, a new concept in building appeared. Arthur Lodge was part of the first villa development, Newington Estate, which was based on the model of Regent's Park in London. Each villa was intended to realise 'the desire for a house like a country gentleman, but more modest and closer to the life of the town'. Every house had its own good garden, shared avenues, porter's lodges and gates whose piers remain today. The first residents were prominent citizens who might well have chosen to live in the grander streets of the New Town but were seduced by the Newington Estate development where homes boasted the characteristics of a country house but on a manageable scale.

Arthur Lodge is attributed to the architect Thomas Hamilton, who aspired to design Grecian palaces but ended up building a school for the local authority and a suburban cottage: the former Royal High School and Arthur Lodge. No mean edifices, these, but both clients were ruined by Hamilton's extravagance. When it was finished in 1829 the house was called Salisbury Cottage. Its first owner, Robert Mason, a builder, became a voluntary bankrupt in August 1830 with a long list of creditors including several carters from the quarries at Hailes and Echobank. The City Treasurer, David Cunningham, who had employed Thomas Hamilton on the George IV Bridge and High School projects became its first resident. But it was Major James Arthur, Deputy Inspector General of Army Hospitals in Scotland, who changed the name of the house to Arthur Lodge when he took it on in 1841.

It is said that on a certain day in midsummer the shadow of the summit of Arthur's Seat falls on Arthur Lodge. That hint of some near-mystical link to the landscape seems intensified by the surrounding Scots pine and the form of the neo-Grecian villa so that visitors might for a brief moment rub their eyes and conjure up the Athens of the south. The house's interiors are a fitting memorial to the dedicated and creative partners, Jack Howells and John Pinkerton, who embarked on an informed restoration of Arthur Lodge in 1985 and who, tragically, both died recently.

Jack Howells and John Pinkerton wanted to restore the garden and the two original entrances to Hamilton's unique and sophisticated interior: a south approach for visitors arriving by carriage who progressed through a small hall, up a marble staircase to the central hall or atrium. Family and visitors arriving without transport could use the east entrance leading through a low square hall, infinitely extended by means of complex mirrors in the arches of a coved ceiling, and up a vaulted stair to the atrium. The architect held that the height of a room should vary proportionately to its other two dimensions. Thus no two rooms have the same ceiling height. On the south side he provided two large public rooms, the full height of the house. Behind them lie two storeys of rooms for family use, and, at the rear, three storeys of rooms for servants. The staircase turns through three sides of the central double-glazed atrium to give access to these various levels. Visitors to Arthur Lodge have called the atrium 'highly idiosyncratic', 'uncompromisingly Greek and uncommonly elegant' and 'one of the most interesting in Scotland'. Hamilton's atrium was intended to refer to the houses of classical antiquity in which a spacious central atrium was a principal feature. Gilded sandstone Ionic columns and massive square pillars supporting open arches embellish this remarkable neo-Greek hall.

The restoration of Arthur Lodge faced the Pinkerton and Howells partnership with considerable challenges, some of which were met by their decision to provide the house with a decorative interior scheme leading on logically from the taste of 1829. Firmly of the belief that historic houses should not stand still, 'they are not fossils, after all,' the partners viewed each room as a challenge to their skills, knowledge and research.

The distiller Andrew Usher (and benefactor of the Usher Hall) bought the house in 1896 and his daughter Jane and her artist husband William Burn Murdoch decorated the dining room in elaborate *beaux-arts* style, complete with painted nymphs and plaster roses. Their work had been ruthlessly scraped off by a later owner, leaving an empty shell and, in the absence of architectural drawings or other records, there was scant evidence of the original appearance of the room. The north-facing main bedroom posed challenges too: the floor had collapsed into the room below, the upper part of the marble chimneypiece had disappeared and the fourteen-feet high ceiling had been painted 'the colour of an Edinburgh bus'.

The Pinkerton-Howells' investigations revealed clues in the dining room. There had once been classical overdoors and a heavy plaster cornice, which were recreated in 1986 to Jack Howells' designs with woodwork by Messrs Brown and Gaff and plasterwork by Mr Cummings. A screen of Ionic pilasters and a red marble chimneypiece, saved from a skip by the Edinburgh New Town Conservation Committee, were installed. In the segmental arch of the ceiling, originally intended for a painting, Alasdair Macleod was commissioned to portray a *trompe l'oeil* Scottish–Greek fantasy, *The Apotheosis of Lord Byron*. After the floor had been reinstated in the bedroom, central heating installed, and a bathroom created in the dressing room, Alasdair Macleod returned to paint a scene of classical Edinburgh with Thomas Hamilton's High School on Calton Hill and the completed Parthenon. The sources of his inspiration, suggested by Jack Howells, included the secondary temple on the Acropolis, the Erechtheum, and a vividly-illustrated book depicting French Empire wallpapers. To increase the illusion of the classical scene behind a screen of Ionic columns, parts of the colonnade have been painted to trick the eye into seeing three dimensions. The bedroom ceiling, too, is *trompe l'oeil*.

Even as Arthur Lodge was under construction, Sir Walter Scott was already knee-deep in his love of antiquity and the picturesque approach at Abbotsford. 'The Georgian period ends with Sir Walter Scott harping on lost glories,' comments Ian Gow, 'and although Scott's taste tends to be solely identified with Abbotsford, his Border home, which is idiosyncratic to the point of eccentricity, it is less well known that one of his protégés, the young house-painter David Ramsay Hay, went on to become an important pioneer interior decorator, the 'arbiter of elegance north of the Tweed', employed in England and Ireland as well as Scotland.'

Scott masterminded the first visit of a British monarch for 171 years. Charles I had been treated to a tableau representing the royal lineage and in 1822 George IV was kitted out as 'Chief of Chiefs' in the kilt, which had been banned after the 1745 rising. Scott's immensely popular first novel, *Waverley*, had been set in 1745. No longer happy to accept the tag 'North British', Scott and 'middling-sort' Scots were on the hunt for a more satisfying identity which would culminate in the 'tartan menace' and 'kailyard' of the Victorian period.

Newhailes's baroque splendour has remained intact, though faded, ever since Sir James Dalrymple added the finishing touches to new apartments after his father's death in 1721. The house escaped the disfigurement of 'Victorianisation' that many Georgian houses were subjected to and its interiors remain virtually as they were in the eighteenth century. A view of the dining room shows the screen of Ionic columns carved by William Strachan with carved lion heads and Greek key pattern frieze and gilded shells, a bevelled Vauxhall plate looking-glass and landscapes by James Norie. Accounts exist for work carried out in the State Diningroom under Sir James Dalrymple. Examples include a note of payment to William Strachan for the carving of the columns in 1734: 'To one pair of Ionick Capitolls fronting 2 ways. 1.12.0.' In 1739 to James Norie: 'To painting at

Newhailes the Dinning (room) Olive Collour. 2.5.4'. The marble-topped side table is decorated with a carved Greek pattern which matches the dado decoration and the column screens.

Daniel Millar of Glasgow supplied a set of mahogany doors decorated with gilded nautical door furniture to Sir James Dalrymple in 1742. A tiny cockleshell hides the keyhole. 'A procession of rooms', typical of classical Georgian house interiors, lies behind the door and culminates in the intimate closet.

A letter from Henry Cheere suggests that Sir James Dalrymple was not entirely happy with the design of the veined marble chimneypiece with its exhausted looking lion. Its proportions, however, balance William Strachan's rococo gilded plasterwork decoration of the portrait surround: garlanded fruits and flowers suspended from masks and elaborated scallop shells. Sir James bought the portrait of his uncle, the first Earl of Stair, by Sir John Medina for four-and-a-half guineas in 1739.

William Dalrymple was in Canton in the 1770s and probably sent this Chinese lacquerwork cabinet back to Newhailes. Long before electric heating was available, footstools were provided to allow guests to keep their feet above draughts while dining.

Allan Ramsay's portrait of Agnes Murray Kynnynmond above the chimneypiece in the Winter Sitting Room. Like all the rococo marble chimneypieces in the grand rooms at Newhailes, it is English and almost certainly from the Cheere workshops in London.

No one really expected a royal guest overnight, but in grand 18th century homes like Newhailes, apartments were kept ready just in case. This closet, a mysterious hidden room off the Bedchamber, would once have sheltered a collection of small precious objects to be shown to visitors.

Magnificent gilded woodwork by William
Strachan and a suitable white marble
chimneypiece with an elegant gilded
overmantle mirror grace the now-
forlorn Bedchamber. Like the other
main rooms of Newhailes it is
remarkably unsullied by the artifacts of
later generations. The original bed has
gone, the red bedspread is 20th century,
but otherwise Sleeping Beauty might
have slept here under the metal-bar
glazed late-18th century windows.

Blair Adam, Kinross-shire, once the home of Georgian Scotland's most eminent architectural family, William Adam and his sons, John, Robert and James. William Adam built the family home which has been described as 'no more than a glorified farmhouse' in 1730 and while father and sons created architectural glories from Hopetoun and Culzean in Scotland to Osterley and Syon in England, Blair Adam itself 'just grow'd'. Today, uniquely among the homes of the great British architects, Blair Adam remains in the ownership of William Adam's descendants. It was John Adam who inherited the house and lands at Blair Adam on William's death in 1748. An able architect, though with little of the spectacular genius of his brother Robert, John gradually took on the overmantle of a landed gentleman with commercial interests. He settled down to improve the estate by landscaping and draining and added an Aberdeen granite quarrying company and a stake in the newly formed Carron Iron Works to his father's considerable commercial legacy. Later, he was almost ruined by his younger brothers' ambitious, though financially disastrous, residential and commercial development in London, the Adelphi. 'They reduced me in a manner to a crumb,' he lamented. He managed to hold on to Blair Adam although he was unable to develop the estate in the style he must have envisaged appropriate to a man of his social standing. 'Economy in the strictest sense is the only thing that can restore us with honour and credit,' John implored in a letter to Robert and James. He was forced to mortgage the estate and once even had to put it on the market. William, John and his son William are immortalised at Blair Adam, in portraits and on a monument erected in a romantic glade near the walled garden. Robert Adam, whose style is still celebrated and emulated throughout the world, and his shadowy brother John, hardly got a look-in at family celebrations. 'Their arduous attempts at striking great strokes testified by The Adelphi, kept them incessantly in difficulty,' wrote their nephew William. 'They died bachelors, so here their history ends.' Blair Adam had deteriorated badly by the mid 1970s when Keith Adam and his wife Elizabeth moved there to begin a labour of love involving the restoration of the house and the walled garden as well as papers of Robert and James which are held in the Blair Adam archives.

House of Dun plasterwork: Joseph Enzer's work (1742–3) is the glory of Dun. The figuration is complex and allegorical with cryptic Jacobite allusions and has been interpreted by John Hardy, who says of the over decoration of one of the hearths in the banqueting room, depicting Mars and a watchful lion: 'Mars, who supported the Romans in war, recalls the Earl of Mar's role as Sword Bearer to the King of Scotland. While the Scottish lion appears 'couchant guardant' (crouching and watching), Mars stands 'guardant' above the Scottish regalia, flanked by nationalistic emblems which refer to the 'Auld Alliance' between Scotland and France, the 'Grand Alliance' between Scotland, England and the Holy Roman Empire and the Union badge created following the 1707 Union of the Scottish and English Parliaments.'

Drawing after Robert Adam's design for the remodelled north front of Yester House, East Lothian.

The Great Drawing Room at Blair Castle, Perthshire: 1758 design for the 2nd Duke of Atholl, by Steuard Mackenzie. Two large landscape paintings, two overdoor 'landskips', two full-length portraits, two pedimented busts, three ornately gilded oblong mirrors, each with a matching sidetable, a double-storied chimneypiece with upper part in the same marble framing a 'cheerfull' looking glass, a festoon of drapery over the casement windows: this is the interior decoration suggested in the design for the Great Drawing Room, the grandest and principal reception room of the castle. Furnishings were seen as part of the architecture of a room; the architect often designed the furniture, and the *objets d'art* would be specially commissioned for the room. Chairs and sofas were placed against the walls and would be covered in the same silk damask as the walls.

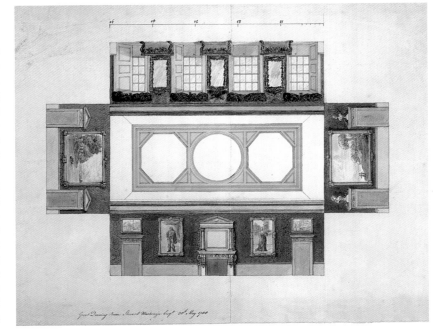

The Library at Arniston House, Midlothian, designed by William Adam c.1726, *Vitruvius Scoticus*, Plate 41. Exploded room design from Adam's splendid publication which depicts the use of classical orders in interiors which emulate the façades of his buildings. The design for the library is all the more ambitious, and uniquely Scottish, situated as it is in the 'skied' attic of Arniston House. Adam achieved this by breaking into the roof space. An order of Ionic capitals with a pulvinated, or bulging, frieze sets out the controlling geography of the room. Each section contains either chimneypiece, or glass-fronted library cupboard, or casement and is finished with eighteen busts of authors. Portrait sculptures were usual in libraries of grand Scottish houses. The room today is grained to imitate oak. *Vitruvius Scoticus*, designed to promote William Adam's architectural achievements, was not published until 1812 and a modern edition followed in 1980.

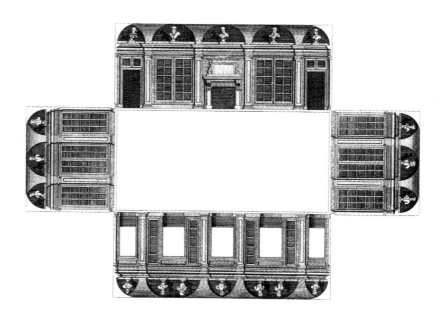

Design for a carpet by Alexander Nasmyth.

Drawing for a decorative panel at Newliston by David Allan.

The partly panelled study of this flat in Chessels Court was probably the dining room when it was first finished about 1745 by the architect and wright Alexander Chessels. Woodwork and plaster work combine to give an impression of solid richness. The chinmneypiece's pulvinated frieze is carved with bay leaves. On the overmantel above is a boldly modelled stucco relief of weapons dangling from a ribbon. The cornice's egg and dart motif is repeated on a smaller scale at the shutter's panels—an expensive touch of class showing that this was the flat's most important room. The overmantel painting in the bedroom was probably executed by James Norie about 1745. The ruins of an improbable building set in a landscape with a city in the distance are Continental themes. The execution is provincial rather than Parisian; but this was not intended as great art. Its prevailing greys and greens ensured that it took its place in the overall decoration of the room rather than standing out as an assertive statement.

Northumberland Place: in the 1980s the late Willie Maclaren took Georgian precedents to extremes by painting the sitting room of his own New Town flat triumphantly *trompe l'oeil*. Maclaren was a painter who moved into this small flat, owned for most of its hundred and eighty years' existence by ministers of the Church of Scotland. John Gifford visited him there and observed 'all traces of Calvinistic gloom have now been dispelled by a virtuoso exhibition of the skill in *trompe l'oeil* decoration which brought him commissions to work at such famous houses as Hopetoun and Tyninghame as well as the Royal Lyceum Theatre. In his sitting room nothing is quite what it seems. The dark scarlet veined marble of the chimneypiece and the purple marble of the obelisks which stand above it are both products of the paintbrush. So too is the wall panelling with its carved shells, swags of flowers and drapery and curvy broken pediment above the door. Even the cords, from which hang the 18th century prints, are painted, but the Venus de Milo in the corner is three-dimensional.'

The dining room of this early 19th century house in Heriot Row was redecorated in the late 1980s as part of the architect's brief to restore the house to its former splendour. The walls are covered with dark green watered silk fabric, the woodwork and cornice painted a soft white. The end wall is an apsed recess (the doors curve in line with the walls) and filled as originally intended with a late Georgian sideboard under a carved and gilded pier glass, probably French, which reflects the light from the windows.

Scotland Street: the parlour of this 1830s flat (William IV rather than strictly Georgian) is dominated by the magnificent glass gasolier (gas was introduced into Edinburgh in 1818 and became widespread in the 1820s). Attached to a white marble chimneypiece (out of picture) carved with Empire garlands is an adjustable firescreen, with a gilded overmantel mirror above, its frame carved with scrolls and a central anthemion. The sofa and chairs are all covered in a yellow damask as was the standard practice of the early 19th century. Against the long wall behind stands a huge mahogany bookcase, perhaps a product of Trotter's cabinet works. On the other wall, a sideboard displays blue and white china.

This house in Danube Street was built in the 1820s and first occupied by a lawyer, perhaps attracted by the promise that the buildings here were 'elegant in their Architecture; substantial in their finishing, and complete in their accommodation'. Concern for the room's architectural detail is emphasised by the choice of festoon blinds in spotted cream silk which shows off rather than conceals the elegantly detailed window architraves. The windows reveal a typical cast-iron balcony of this part of the New Town, of honeysuckle and lattice design. The wallcovering is a stipple-effect paper in deep pink. The white marble chimneypiece and hanging cabinet hold a collection of china with pride of place given to a Newhall teapot and Chinese bowl. The elegant chandelier was purchased in recent times from a New Town antique shop.

An appropriate obelisk and pair of 18th-century French gilded wood sphinxes displayed on an inlaid mahogany and satinwood secretaire made at Maybole, Ayrshire, around 1790. A watercolour view of the south side of Edinburgh and George Heriot's Hospital from the Castle Rock by Ann Stewart, 1811, hangs on the ragworked wall.

Mahogany longcase clock *c.*1830 made by James Hunter of Johnstone near Paisley. The spandrils depict the seasons and the painted scene shows Lowlanders and Highlanders in vigorous dispute.

Neo-classical settee or daybed, painted and grained beech frame simulating rosewood with lyre decorative motif. Typical of early 19th century craftsmanship, possibly by Trotter, Young and Hamilton, designed to 'leaven English Regency elegance with Scottish dignity and give value for money'. William Trotter's aim was to provide his customers with what they wanted to possess.

As in all contemporary restorations of historic interiors, compromises have to be made and sometimes rooms are created anew. The kitchen of the Georgian House at 7 Charlotte Square, Edinburgh, was an empty shell when The National Trust for Scotland set about reinstating it. Now it is every bit as popular with visitors as the grander rooms of the model Georgian House on the floors above. Tinware would have been more appropriate than copper and the salvaged open range should have winding cheeks, 'but beggars can't be choosers,' says the curator who had in mind 'a quite modest family, just able to afford the address and bringing their old belongings with them' when he recreated the kitchen for them in the basement. He imagines the family might have had a staff of cook, kitchen maid and tablemaid who worked in an atmosphere of 'workmanlike clutter' where stone flags, scrubbed wood table and heavy utensils were familiar features. To some extent the curator's hunch was confirmed by the discovery in 1983 of watercolours by Mary Ellen Best depicting late Georgian interiors and a kitchen in particular 'simply sagging with pewter'. Some of the curator's own inspirations add 'texture' rather than absolute authenticity and delight visitors, always an important challenge for The National Trust: the sugar cone, ready for pestle and mortar pounding, is a favourite with visitors as are the hams and pheasants which appear ready for preparation. The open range was salvaged from a skip near the curator's office in Young Street. Patented in 1802, ranges like this, with simmering, steaming and roasting capacity, were not widely used in Scotland until the 20th century. Several items in the room were restored at the Trust's workshops: the candelabra, the range screen, a bread oven rescued from under the main railway line at East Linton. The fine late 18th-century hotplate came from the former house of Admiral Duncan in George Square and the large dripping pan was found in an Edinburgh junk shop. The walls are painted with an authentic blue paint which was thought to keep flies at bay.

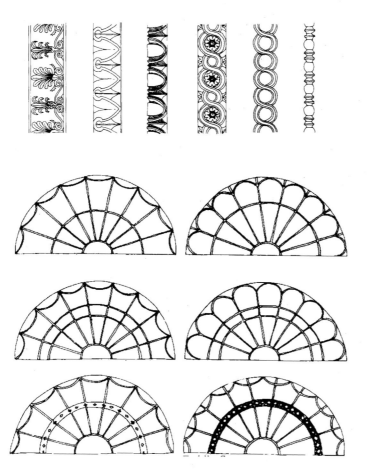

Patterns taken from *The Care and Conservation of Georgian Houses* : fanlight windows and designs for use in carving, plasterwork and metalwork: anthemion and palmette, leaf and dart, egg and dart, elaborate guilloche, plain guilloche, bead and reel.

Anthemion and palmette design for cast-iron balcony at Moray Place, Edinburgh.

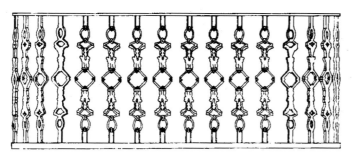

Design for a cast-iron balcony at Leith Street, Edinburgh.

Above cliffs and goblin-haunted caves, Robert Adam engaged in a twenty year programme of enlargement and improvement which incorporated and concealed the old towerhouse of the Cassillis family and produced a dazzling new building in his castle style. Alexander Nasmyth's panoramas, which hang in the picture room, vividly portray Culzean Castle's dramatic cliff-top perch.

The late Colin McWilliam, lived at Culzean during the 1960s and, later, imagined a guest arriving to see the interiors: 'and what an adventure to reach them! A guest on a Georgian evening would have come down the long drive past Hoolity Ha' Lodge, under the ruined arch and along the causeway, then up to the forecourt, with a moonlit prospect of the Clyde and Ailsa Craig over the battlements.'

The National Trust for Scotland accepted Culzean in 1945 but it was not until 1972 that the first radical restoration by the curatorial team got under way. The restoration was based on knowledge of the buildings and its surviving fittings and furnishings as well as extensive research. A collection of Adam drawings in Sir John Soane's Museum revealed the original intention of the architect. They also indicated the colour palette Adam selected for ceilings and other plasterwork. The eating room now functions as a sitting room. Colin McWilliam paid tribute to the original: 'How magical to have dined there, between the dynamic symmetry of the two curved ends, under one of the wittiest of all late Adam ceilings!'

A view through the Corinthian columns of the first floor, across the elliptical staircase and into the round saloon at Culzean Castle, the most extensive and dramatic demonstration of the castle style which Robert Adam developed for wealthy patrons during the last twenty-five years of his life. In May 1787 he initialled a set of plans for an elliptical, top-lit staircase to be inserted at the centre of Culzean Castle, then the seat of David Kennedy, 10th Earl of Cassillis. From a modest entrance hall, rather casually, a door opens into the elliptical stair-well, surely the most spectacular of Robert Adam's conjuring tricks, as Colin McWIlliam said. 'Dimly lit by our standards it must have seemed of colossal height (exaggerated by the low handrail) and extraordinary grandeur, reaching its climax with the Corinthian columns of the first floor. For effective contrast Adam used smaller Ionic columns for the upper storey beneath the cupola (a daring inversion of classical practice) and also for the visitor's lateral progress through a vestibule into the great round saloon.'

Arthur Lodge: Thomas Hamilton's 'Grecian dream house' was restored recently, thanks to the devotion of the late Jack Howells and John Pinkerton. Both have died since these photographs were taken and are much missed. The house was part of the first villa development, Newington Estate, which was modelled on the Regent's Park, London, development. Each villa had its own garden and was intended to realise 'the desire for a house like a country gentleman, but more modest and closer to the life of the town'. Shared avenues, porters' lodges and gates (which were closed by midnight) enhanced the fantasy of living on a country estate.

The entrance hall, with domed and mirrored ceiling, marble floor and entrance screen, was embellished and altered by the Usher family in 1899. Early 19th-century busts of prominent figures, including Lord Cockburn, Sir John Ross and the Marquis of Huntly, preside over the hall which gives access to an arched marble staircase leading to the great central hall or atrium of the original house.

The neo-classical dining room restored: salvaged columns were stripped and marbled 'rouge royale' to match the chimneypiece. The anthemion and palmette cornice frieze was cast from an original tile section from Dunmore Park. The Greek-revival furniture includes a side table from Keir House. Casts of the carved anthemion and rosette decoration of the side-table were copied to embellish the mirror above. The walls are painted French grey and hung with a collection of 18th-century engravings. Neo-classical figures (after Canova) were found, thickly over-painted, in an Edinburgh junk shop and restored to grace the room. The *trompe l'oeil* ceiling, *The Apotheosis of Lord Byron* depicts Scotland's National Bard and Saint Andrew greeting Byron's chariot, pulled by heroes of the Greek Wars, at the portals of Heaven (the Scottish Assembly building on Calton Hill).

An Ionic screen, a *trompe l'oeil* mural painted by Alasdair Macleod, runs round the bedroom fronting views of the Athens of the North including The Palace of Holyroodhouse. Thomas Hamilton's masterpiece, the Scottish Assembly building under Calton Hill, is depicted with the saltire flying as if a National Assembly was in session. 'Edinburgh's Disgrace', the Parthenon on the Calton Hill, is shown tranformed as the finished National Monument, the Chapel Royal of Holyroodhouse is roofed and restored, the state bed at Arthur Lodge stands ready, on a carpeted dias, for a royal guest. The bed dias, under its high 1800s French style canopy, was still evolving when this picture was taken: a bed surround embellished with caryatids and a crown of white ostrich feathers were added later.

The dining room chimneypiece was salvaged by the Edinburgh New Town Conservation Committee. The two classical figures are by the Danish sculptor Thorvaldsen; the French clock is Second Empire. The overmantel mirror reflects the restored doorcases based on a Thomas Hamilton design.

Self-portrait by John Kay, Barber and Caricaturist *c.* 1785: this is much more than a self-portrait of John Kay. The painting also reveals a great deal about the interior he inhabited. The details of the rooms (a glimpse is given into an adjoining room) show that although they seem sparsely furnished everything is elegantly finished in the manner of the day. The wooden shutters are panelled simply, the fringed swag of a velvet window-hanging is just visible, the mahogany matching chairs are brass studded. The door frame is painted in two shades of what appears to be olive green, the darker shade repeating the wall colouring, and the dentil cornice and skirting of the inner room are painted a fresh light colour. The carpet might be of Scottish manufacture. Ian Gow suggests that the neat pattern built up by the careful hanging of the prints and oval miniatures in the inner room is probably less a record of an actual decor than an allusion to Kay's profession and prolific output of etchings and portraits.

Midfield Cottage, 1807: Mr and Mrs Campbell with Lady Molesworth and Miss Brown in the Drawing Room at Midfield Cottage, Lasswade, Midlothian, by Alexander Carse, 1807. The painting is the first detailed record of the interior of an actual room in Scottish art yet discovered. This charming summer scene might be Edwardian in its atmosphere of lightness and accomplishment, reflected in the open windows, the airiness of the space, the piano, the harp and the informal arrangement of the furniture. Alas, the Victorian age lay round the corner and rooms like this would become over-stuffed and cluttered. For the time being, the three sisters and their host give every impression of enjoying their thatched cottage orné in the new villa development near the banks of the River Esk. The ceiling of the oval-shaped room is embellished simply with a leaf cornice and the walls are painted one colour in line with Robert Adam's recommendations for simple neo-classical interiors. Ian Gow has remarked that the chimneypiece has

been identified as one which came from an Edinburgh workshop, but the maker has not been identified. It is probably marbled to match the real marble slabs of the inner frame. The fitted carpet appears to be flat-woven in a simple geometric design. It is a transitional interior which reveals the will of the owners in the softening of the architectural features of the windows, for example, with several draped layers and, even more radical, the furniture, which in a classical Georgian interior would have been ranged against the walls, has been pulled out to serve the comfort and convenience of the room's inhabitants. 'A clutter of objects spread about the room creates a deliberately 'lived-in' look and relaxed atmosphere in contrast to more formal early Georgian habits,' observes Ian Gow. 'And a new breed of light tables, like the worktable, could be easily moved without the intervention of servants. The pile of books on the chimneypiece, the most important item and focal point of an early Georgian interior, would have seemed shockingly casual to a former generation.'

Sir Walter Scott's Abbotsford, 1820, exemplifies the Picturesque approach to architecture dominant at the time. Lockhart, his biographer, noted: 'Sir Walter abominated the commonplace daubing of walls, panels, and doors with coats of white, blue or grey and thought that sparklings or edgings of gilding only made their baldness or poverty more noticeable'. Sir Walter loved recherché carving and a collection of antique oak carvings ornamented the Hall (not shown) where David Ramsay Hay, Scott's house-painter protégé imitated the grain and tone on what Ian Gow calls the 'glaring white gimcrack paster vault'. Hay recorded that he was instructed to make his painting work 'appear somewhat weather-beaten and faded, as if it had stood untouched for many years', and to tone down the real modern oak of the door and shutter linings to blend with it. 'Having painted the most famous house in Europe to his patron's satisfaction, Hay went on to become the most fashionable decorator in Scotland. A repertoire of rich theatrical effects had entered the decorator's vocabulary through the Gothic revival and its lessons were soon to be applied to every style.' The new interior style became beloved by the Victorian age and supplanted, in modish homes at least, the Adamesque.

The Chaplain's Parlour at Trinity College Hospital, Edinburgh, by William Douglas, 1845: Trinity College Hospital, with its important medieval chapel, was demolished by Victorian 'improvers' to make way for the present Waverley Station in 1845. The Reverend John Sime who occupied this room was heartbroken and commissioned this view on the very eve of the Hospital's destruction. Sime was an antiquarian who devoted his leisure to recording Scotland's ancient buildings and the room preserves the spirit of a mid-Georgian interior. A companion painting, showing the room of the Hospital's matron, shows that she had 'succumbed to every fashionable whim' says Ian Gow, 'whereas Sime's only concession to the 19th century is the gas-mantle in its conventional place on the centre of the chimneypiece. All the furniture, which is at least eighty years old, is lined up against the walls 18th-century style and the reefed curtains follow a 1780 fashion which became outmoded in the Regency period. The coffered Neo-classical-pattern of the flatwoven carpet had been superseded by a preference for naturalistic floral bouquets. There is no useless bric-a-brac.' A Carron Iron Works grate stands in the chimneypiece with brass fender and fire irons.

William Bonar's dining room at East Warriston House, Edinburgh, in a painting by Miss Bonar c.1840: Alexander Carse's interiors, such as the painting of Midfield Cottage, influenced amateur artists in the second quarter of the 19th century to emulate him. Here Miss Bonar has faithfully recorded the family dining room at East Warriston House, built around 1820 as a villa standing in its own grounds with large Venetian windows facing south, and panoramic views of the city. The stone entrance piers are visible today, opposite the entrance to the offices of the Royal Botanical Garden. The room in the painting straddles two eras, uneasily displaying features of both. Dining room interior decoration usually lagged behind more fashionable drawing room interiors: they had to be practical and convenient, the carpets, often a geometric Turkey pattern, were usually unfitted. Ian Gow suggests that the Bonar dining room, with its fitted carpet, might have doubled as the sitting room allowing the drawing room to closed up to preserve its more costly and fragile contents, except when the family was entertaining. The walls have been treated with plaster panelling , the latest New Town vogue, and plain-painted. The landscape paintings in their heavy gilt frames should properly be suspended from a picture rail. The paintings, the heavy red tablecovers and matching drapery forced across the arch-topped window, announce, already, Victoria's age. In 1848 Frederic Chopin stayed with a Polish doctor in Warriston Crescent nearby and in 1850, the year Chopin died in Paris, Robert Louis Stevenson was born at 9 Howard Place, a stone's throw from East Warriston House.

CASTLE AND CROFT
1830–1900

'Tartanry' was substitute history, but a serious

search for Scotland's past was again under way

Entrance porch to the croft, at
12 Lower Ardelve, Kintail.

L

ady Augusta Bruce noted in her 1855 diary: 'the carpets are Royal Stewart and green Hunting Stewart, the curtains . . . lined with red . . . and a few chintz with a thistle pattern, the chairs and sofas in the drawing room are Dress Stewart poplin. All highly characteristic and appropriate, but not all equally *flatteux* to the eye.' She referred to Balmoral, which Queen Victoria built in baronial style in 1848 and decorated accordingly. Lord Rosebery, one of 'a parade of British politicians forced to make the long, late-summer train journey to Deeside for a royal audience,' considered the drawing room to be the ugliest room in the world. But, as Michael Lynch comments, the very 'Scottishness of Balmoral helped to give the monarchy a truly British dimension for the first time. It had discovered a new popularity, which intertwined and camouflaged the conflicting identities of a Scottish nation with a British state . . . A new, sanitised version of Scottishness emerged – in the minds, at least, of Lowlanders and tourists.'

There were other influences at work shaping Victorian interiors as an astonishing variety of housing spawned across the social spectrum. A cross-section of these interiors is represented here in archive photographs from the collection of the National Monuments Record of Scotland and in recent interior photographs of Mount Stuart, grandest of Victorian homes; of Ayton Castle in Berwickshire, one of the first and best of baronial mansion-castles; of Cardy House in Lower Largo, the middle-class villa of a self-made man; of The National Trust for Scotland's Fyvie Castle and the Glasgow Tenement House; and of 12 Lower Ardelve, Kintail, which was Scotland's last inhabited thatched croft house until the recent death of its owner.

Closer to our own times, the homes of Victorians, as well as their attitudes and aspirations, are easier imaginatively to reconstruct and understand than those of any previous age as, for the first time, photography as well as a wealth of historical documents recorded actual interiors. Photography harnesses conjecture to a reality which was previously inaccessible, except for a few examples of pictorial representation of interiors in the coloured plans of William Adam and other architects of the previous century, and a few paintings such as those of Alexander Carse. As the wealthy exploiters of Victorian invention, technology, innovation and industry ordered up castles and country houses from the successful architects of the day, cities burgeoned with housing for the new breed of middle-class professionals as well as for the workers who served the new industries. The nineteenth century was the age of the city. From the 1830s, spaciously planned urban developments of crescents and circuses were laid out west of Glasgow, while south of the Clyde, superior suburbs sprang up downwind of industry. 'The first of them, Pollockshields, shows a very different taste from the classical circuses and crescents north of the river,' says Elizabeth Williamson describing David Rhind's 1849 development as 'more loosely picturesque, with roads lined with villas following the contours of the hills'. Villa suburbs such as Perth Road, Dundee, and Newington and Trinity, Edinburgh, pre-dated Pollockshields. A few salubrious Glasgow suburbs sprouted on land purchased by businessmen round clusters of Georgian country villas and all the leafy suburbs swelled later in the century with the advent of trams and the suburban railway.

The industrial suburbs were a different matter: street after street of gaunt tenements provided for workers associated with the coal and iron ore industries deterred the affluent from moving east, north and south of the Clyde. Model industrial settlements were attempted at Cowlairs for railway workers, at Possilpark for Saracen Foundry employees, and similar planned communities, some philanthropic, appeared at Scotstoun, Jordanhill and Springburn. 'By far the greatest amount of non-speculative housing for the artisan class (it was too expensive for the poorest) was built by the City Improvement Trust as part of its huge programme of Urban Renewal,' comments Elizabeth Williamson. These 'respectable' tenements were designed with a room and kitchen, each with a box bed, or as 'single ends' with room and kitchen combined. And variations on the tenement theme erupted throughout Scotland on the back of industry, in cities and new towns such as Greenock and Paisley and shanty towns like Blantyre and the Monklands. Shared privies were in the communal courtyard, or back green, until 1892 regulations ordered them inside.

Glasgow's middle-class tenements had bathrooms as early as 1830. Some were as sophisticated as London's mansion flats and, by the end of the century, their owners had begun to refer to them as 'mansions' in distinction to the less desirable tag of 'tenement'. Charing Cross Mansions is a superior example with a 'French Second Empire façade' while round the corner at 145 Buccleuch Street, four simple apartments constituted what is now The National Trust for Scotland's Tenement House.

From the beginning of the century, Glasgow's industrial revolution had been fuelled by plentiful supplies of cheap labour: migrants from the Highlands and immigrants from Ireland. Almost a quarter of a million Highlanders lived in Glasgow, working in cotton mills, railway construction and, seasonally, on Lowland farms. Among their number were the ancestors of Donald Mackenzie of 12 Lower Ardelve who brought back coins bearing the head of George III, which were later mounted on a piece of varnished wood from Donald's boat. The inscription read: '1812: Tokens for lodgings given in Glasgow to men from the Highlands who came to give their labour in the Industrial Revolution and leave their mark in shipbuilding and engineering that exists to this day.'

The house they and Donald inhabited is a listed building, now under the care of Historic Scotland; its rare and precious thatching maintained by *Cairdean nan Taighean Tugha* (Friends of the Thatched Houses). 12 Lower Ardelve is an empty shell now, but wind and water-tight, clinging to the very earth, like some ancient prehistoric broch. For a century-and-a-half the seasons have come and gone, winter to spring, spring to summer, and summer to those glorious autumns which illuminate the hills of Kintail with golden brown fern laced with soft purple heather, and entwine houses like this in a bower of red rowan and honeysuckle berries. Peering through the windows I see that all signs of human life have gone from the place: the parlour dresser which once overflowed with treasured mementos, plates, cruets, jugs, egg-cups and the like as well as essential items of Donald Mackenzie's life: a Bible, alarm clock, torch, binoculars, bills and letters. The plates and jugs have been cleared off adjoining shelves where a toby jug shared space with special china including one or two Oriental items, and a set of six cups and saucers commemorating the coronation of George VI. Gone is the cut paper shelf-edging with a rose pattern which blended with the poppy-motif wallpaper. Nothing remains in the bedroom where portraits of Donald Mackenzie's parents hung above the bed opposite a printed oil-cloth map of Scotland; not even the chest of drawers, once the repository of prints, pictures, wash jug and basin, starched collars and a black homburg for Church attendance.

This is how dwellings, through time, become monuments, rare survivals, representative in the case of Donald's croft, of thousands of other thatched houses whose fate is to have become mere rickles of stones, memorial piles to well-founded but arduous and poverty-stricken lives. When I visited him in 1986, Donald told me that his father and his father before him lived here, and the boys who brought back the coins before that. If you consider that Donald's father was born in 1856, that's going back a bit. Season after season the house has resisted the changes which time had impressed on other croft houses (ruins or heaps of rubble on the landscape) leaving this, the only thoroughbred: a fact made final in 1974 when an official preservation order dropped through the door stating that 12 Lower Ardelve was now a listed building. Thus, just as Donald might have been getting round to making a few changes, fate decreed otherwise. But, as he pointed out, number 12 was as important in its own way as the sovereign's residence at Balmoral.

Donald Mackenzie was given the same name as his father who married Isabella Macrae, daughter of Donald Macrae of Camas-luinie which is situated several miles up the valley above Ardelve. Their portraits hung in the bedroom beside that of the Revd Dr Angus Galbraith, Free Church Minister of Lochalsh at the time. It was as if, grouped together, their collective image still exerted an influence to keep things as they were meant to be. The Free Church came into being in 1843 and although a few things have changed since that momentous day, when Donald invited me to look inside I understood that the interior of the thatched house was not so different from how it always had been.

At the fireside he conjured up memories and stories of crofting days which were over for him now; past eighty years old, yet he still rode a bicycle to exercise his arthritic knee. He explained that a single chimney set in the centre of the room once sent the smoke up a through a central hole in the roof. Later, two fireplaces were constructed with wooden chimneys in the gable ends. This was one, where we sat, a hanging lum, a near-unique survival. Wood was the fuel now, instead of peat which Donald remembered being set, damp blocks to the back of the fire, dry to the front, under the all-purpose Dutch oven which his mother baked in. He demonstrated with his hands how she lifted hot ashes onto its lid to cook the top of rounds of scones. And she produced slow-simmered soups and stews too, though herring and potatoes were the mainstay of the family diet.

He himself cooked on a Calor gas stove, a fact which made him recount with relish the time in the 1950s when 'the Hydro' was inciting, as he put it, crofters like him to convert to electric. 'They sent a photographer down and got two villagers to dress up as removal men and snapped them carrying in a brand-new cooker as if it were for them. They got as far as the door, took the snap and carried the cooker back to the van. We couldn't afford one! My niece joked about grabbing the stove off them and locking it inside. But, unfortunately, that was the last we heard of cooking stoves – until I went to the Highland Show at Inverness. There was the photograph all over the place with us in it! And we were still on the Calor. It was all just propaganda!'

Five children were brought up in the two rooms of 12 Lower Ardelve. The children slept in the bedroom and his parents slept in a box bed pulled down at night and placed between the parlour window and the fireplace. A corrugated iron porch was added later to take a stone sink. The front windows look directly over panoramic views of Loch Duich and Eilean Donan Castle which Donald recalls being rebuilt when he was a boy, around 1913. One tiny window to the back gives a peep out of the closet to the hills and the land behind the croft which once supported crops and vegetables in season, ducks, hens, a few cows, a horse and a pony whose most important function was to carry down the peats which the whole family went to cut from peat banks on the hills five miles away. They fished, too, for saith, ling, cod and herring which they salt-cured, some for themselves and some for others, selling half-a-barrel of several hundred fish to families in the hills. Each year, to enrich the croft land, rafts of seaweed were towed in to the shores of the loch and set in piles to be rainwashed for fertiliser.

Either the family was too large to support the boys who left home for Glasgow and brought back the coins, and the crofting land too small to support them, or their own ambitions led them out into the world where their lives might well have been brutish and short. As Michael Lynch observes: 'Life in the mid-Victorian city was far from tranquil, but it was not afflicted by the violent anarchy which could overtake settlements clustered near mines or iron works . . . there violence, strikes and industrial intimidation – by both employers and fellow workers – added extra hazards to life.'

On the other side of the fence, the burgeoning middle classes invested in property and the richest set up as landed gentry, emulating the elaborate codes of behaviour of the older 'upper classes' which, as Mark Girouard suggests, 'was partly a defensive sieve or initiatory rite, designed to keep out the wrong people. What to wear when, how to address whom, the ritual of making morning calls and leaving cards – here were plenty of traps for the uninitiated, especially when most of the rules were unwritten.' A Victorian landowner, said the architect George Gilbert Scott, 'has been placed by providence in a position of authority and dignity; and no false modesty should deter him from expressing this, quietly and gravely, in the character of his house.' He referred to *nouveaux riches* and older families alike, who closed ranks as the century progressed and working-class unrest entrenched. The growing cities where the working classes and the poor were segregated into specific areas were like macrocosms of the Victorian household in which the servants were cut off from the lives of the owners as bluntly as architects could devise. Servants were no longer 'part of the family' as in earlier times. Systems of corridors, backstairs, and even tunnels ensured that the embarrassing circumstance of servant and family meeting, except when the staff was serving them directly, happened as rarely as possible. Additionally, the sexes were segregated within the servants' quarters into male zones (the butler's) and female zones (the cook's, housekeeper's and laundry). By the late 1830s at House of Falkland, William Burn (1789–1870) had designed interiors which incorporated the Victorian requirements of efficiency and morality to the highest degree, typically dividing the servants' wing into four areas for butler, cook, housekeeper and laundry. At Newhailes in Victorian times, the laundry staff reached the drying green through a sunken passage, meeting neither grooms nor guests. Robert Kerr, who regarded baronial revival houses 'bedecked with pepper-pot bartisans' as merely the produce of that 'dreary northern kingdom' wrote in *The Gentleman's House* (1856): 'It becomes the foremost of all maxims, therefore, that the Servants' Department shall be separated from the main house, so that what passes on either side of the boundary shall be both invisible and inaudible to the other.' As Girouard comments: 'Kerr's language is rather too reminiscent of the language of apartheid. Separation in Victorian country houses could be carried to uncomfortable limits . . . It is still a disconcerting experience to push through the baize doors studded with brass nails, that divided the servants from the family, and pass from carpets, big rooms, light, comfort and air to dark corridors, linoleum, poky rooms, and the ghostly smell of stale cabbage.' Town houses, too, were segregated from the beginning of the century, the baize door severing dark and dismal servants' basement quarters from the airy rooms above.

As many Highland and Island homes still do, Donald Mackenzie's croft signalled, when it was inhabited, the most momentous event in nineteenth-century Scottish history in the image of the 'Wee Free' minister of his parents' time hanging over the bed, in the black-bound Bible, in the church-going homburg hat and stiff collars. In 1843, after a long statement of protest had been read out 'amid the breathless stillness' to the 2nd Marquis of Bute, Lord High Commissioner of the General Assembly of the Church of Scotland, and, later in the day, a 'Deed of Demission' had been signed by dissenting ministers, roughly one-third left the established church and, soon set up a parallel parochial system with churches and schools. The Disruption was a shattering blow to the Established Church and, throughout the century, religion diversified like society itself and acted as a catalyst in the proliferation of the decorative arts.

John Patrick Crichton Stuart, 3rd Marquis of Bute, was the greatest patron of Victorian architecture and his life at the very top of the social, economic and political ladder was the stuff of Victorian fantasies. Mount Stuart, his Scottish home on the Isle of Bute, was 'a monument to pre-industrial values built from the proceeds of an industrial fortune' based on the exportation of coal from Cardiff. A *palazzo*, really, it is set in parkland formerly grazed by wallabies, which slopes down to the Firth of Clyde, and amid well-tended fields and woodlands. A 'disastrous' fire in 1877, however, necessitated extensive rebuilding of the older house, 'the new house to be reared on the site of the old, incorporating its original north and south wings'. The architect selected to carry out the work was Robert Rowand Anderson who designed new interiors to reflect the passions and wide-ranging interests of Lord Bute, which included architecture, art and design, languages, psychic phenomena and astrology, heraldry, gardening and a wide range of 'causes'. Rowand Anderson chose a firm of Glasgow builders, Watt and Wilson, for the main construction of the house but the artists and decorators who created the stained glass and painterwork harked back to William Burges's influence on the Marquis's other homes at Cardiff Castle and Castell Coch and included Campbell, Smith and Campbell and W. F. Lonsdale.

Ayton Castle in Berwickshire is the finest example of the grand baronial houses which the architect James Gillespie Graham was called upon to construct for *nouveau riche* clients eager to emulate 'old family' values. It is the most prominent of country houses viewed from the east coast Edinburgh to London railway line which cuts a swathe across the 5000 acre estate: a spectacular sight admired every day by countless British Rail passengers. Even visitors approaching by road are struck by Ayton's dominance of the landscape, rather as pilgrims approaching a medieval abbey must have been. From a lofty hilltop site, its dignified sandstone towers signal permanence and authority, though the straightforward baronial exterior offers few clues to its lavish interiors.

David Bryce altered some of Gillespie Graham's interiors in two phases from 1860. W. Mitchell-Innes, the banker who commissioned the house, never lived there and in 1888 the house was purchased from his son by ancestors of the present owner David Liddell-Grainger, a descendant of Richard Grainger, the Newcastle developer dubbed 'the Cubitt of the North'. Mitchell-Innes managed to leave his mark, though, in the pious quasi-heraldic inscription carved over the front door and painted on the ceiling of the entrance hall. Inscriptions and homilies executed in carvings, paint and embroidery became a Victorian speciality: 'Except the Lord Build a House They Labour in Vain that Build It' and 'Home Sweet Home' were favourites. Just over the border at Cragside, Lord Armstrong, the millionaire arms dealer, had 'East or West, Home is Best' inscribed on a fireplace while at Ayton the *nouveau riche* Mitchell-Innes fulsomely announced his *hauteur* in the motto '*Deo Favente*', heedless, perhaps, of the adage: 'Whom the Gods love die young'. Later, the Grainger family, descendants of the present owner, introduced their 'old family' motto, with no trace of false piety 'Valour is stronger than a battering ram'.

The unfortunate Mr Mitchell-Innes's fate hinged less on God's favour than that of his wife, the former Miss Innes, an Edinburgh heiress who married him when he was still a humble bank clerk. He rose swiftly to become a director of a prominent bank but he was caught with his hand in the till of his wife's trust funds after beneficiaries rumbled him to the Edinburgh newspaper, the *Thistle*. Mitchell-Innes bought up the paper in an unsuccessful attempt to silence the scandal which eventually drove him to suicide. By the time he was buried in Ayton cemetery, he had also built houses at Ingliston and Stowe as well as the nearly-finished Ayton Castle.

The castle in its mid-century heyday was run by a fleet of forty servants, including laundry, garden and stable staff. Butler and housekeeper presided over the indoor staff while the head gardener and head groom ruled the outdoor workers. Tending the central heating system which pushed hot air through the corridors, the coal fires and candles in the rooms, the fetching and carrying of water before the house was plumbed later in the century, were tasks that had to be performed several times a day. When, eventually, the house was plumbed, one of Gillespie Graham's towers was commandeered to contain a water tank of 650 gallons capacity supplied, as it is today, from the estate. At the end of the nineteenth century new technology produced two new categories of country house servant: the chauffeur and the electrician. Today, the interiors of Ayton are managed by two part-time local women armed, of course, with the latest technology of which the vacuum cleaner is still the most revolutionary.

'Valour is stronger than a battering ram' is a motto which serves David Liddell-Grainger well, as does the symbol of rams' heads which appear throughout the house carved on furniture and the like and even moulded onto the ends of brass curtain rails. He has been restoring Ayton for years: exteriors in the summer, interiors in the winter; and his informal maxim is, 'If you must restore, go the whole hog'. The frequently absent owners of many other Victorian estates, less inclined to sink dwindling fortunes into their preservation, are witness to crumbling powerhouses, farmhouses and workers' cottages: the Victorian dream, impossible to sustain in the late-twentieth century.

The Glen, Peeblesshire, was built for Charles Tennant from 1852. One of Scotland's six industrialists who made it to the British multi-millionaire league, Charles inherited the St Rollox chemical works founded by his father John Tennant. 'All six had in common the fact that the new urban landscape of Glasgow or its environs was their Elysian fields,' says Michael Lynch; and their country estates were earthly paradises, depending, of course on the weather. William Chambers wrote in 1864 that Glen House was 'one of those magnificent creations of David Bryce in the old Scottish baronial style' which materialised from the architect's kit in many parts of the country. 'The entrance is from a spacious quadrangle on the north, so as to leave the entire southern side with the best apartments towards the sun . . . Within the mansion is demonstrated an extraordinary ingenuity of architectural contrivance – kitchen, larder, and servants' departments, public-rooms, guests' rooms, private family-rooms, business-room, library, billiard-room, smoking-room &c. On the opposite side of the quadrangle is a court environed with stables, possessing all the modern improvements. Beyond, are the gardens, greenhouses, vineries, on an extensive scale, with a tastefully-built farm-steading, and dwellings for gardeners and game-keeper.' The Glen, then as now, was a working farm and sporting estate where the access road forks at the gatehouse and a landscaped drive delivers family and guests smoothly to the 'big house' while a secondary road keeps workers' cottages 'out of sight and out of mind'.

Segregation was practised 'Upstairs' as well as 'Downstairs'. Grand houses had owners' wings including bedrooms, dressing rooms, boudoir and a study. Nursery wings, sometimes with a schoolroom, tended to be separated from, but connected to, parents' quarters. Domains and rituals that were specifically male or female evolved. Morning calls or afternoon calls were enacted with polite conversation between hostesses, and afternoon tea was taken by both sexes in the drawing room or on the lawn, according to the weather. Dining room and drawing room were contrasted by

Robert Kerr as of 'masculine importance' and 'feminine delicacy'; 'which in effect,' comments Girouard, 'usually meant massive oak or mahogany and Turkey carpets in the dining room and spindly gilt or rosewood, and silk or chintz in the drawing room'. Bachelors had their own upstairs quarters, and sometimes even their own entrance and reception hall into the house, and supported the smoking room and billiards room which appeared towards the end of the century.

Very different from grand houses but characteristic of more modest middle-class villas springing up everywhere in cities and towns was the peaceful Fife home built in 1871 for descendants of Alexander Selkirk, the famous castaway upon whom Daniel Defoe based the character of Robinson Crusoe. The village of Lower Largo, where Cardy House is situated, is a picturesque straggle of eighteenth-century weavers' and fishermens' houses running parallel to the seashore in the East Neuk of Fife. But even Cardy House is a mansion compared with the neighbouring cottages and crowstepped pantiled tenements of the village. A Louis revival garden seat invites contemplative repose in a timewarp where concrete classical statues, including a Muse under the apple tree, Atlas supporting the world above the entrance porch and an Arcadian youth loitering in the garden, are only a little the worse for a century's weathering.

The builder of Cardy was David Selkirk Gillies, a great-great-great grandson of Alexander Selkirk. Gillies was born in 1843 and despite little formal education, his drive and business acumen fired the founding of a fishing net factory. He employed sixty local women there when he was only twenty-four years old. A portrait photograph shows this self-made Victorian, aged forty-two, with high domed forehead, thinning hair and dashing Dundreary whiskers. A philanthropist and visionary, the remarkable David Gillies acted as legal adviser to the people of Lower Largo and compiled and preserved the records of the community. When the photographs in this book were taken in 1986, the interiors had scarcely changed since David married Isabella in 1886 and commissioned a Scottish double bed to mark the occasion, with a Gothic upholstered headboard and white damask bedspread both woven with the motif 'Cardy House, Largo' and the couple's initials. And the dining room, set for afternoon tea, had changed little since the Earl and Countess of Aberdeen and their guests sat here with David Gillies after T. Stuart Burnett's statue of Alexander Selkirk, *aka* Robinson Crusoe, was unveiled in the village in 1885. A bronze bust cast from the statue overlooked the entrance hall in Cardy House. But since the house was photographed, the contents have been dispersed and the illustrations in this book now constitute a rare historic record of a Victorian house with the decorative overlay of the original scheme, executed by James Darling of Edinburgh, who was a family friend. Details of James Darling's later wall painting suggest his strong interest in Renaissance painted decoration similar to the work in the bedchamber at Gladstane's Land (see p.45).

Decorative paint effects and stencilling were all the rage towards the end of the century. Stencilling, encouraged by the Gothic Revival of the 1860s, became a popular alternative to printed borders at cornice and dado level. Graining too, was in demand, maple for drawing rooms, oak or walnut for libraries, and mantelpieces were often treated to a coloured marble or grained effect. After 1880 walls tended to be divided into three components: frieze, filling and dado. Embossed papers such as Lincrusta, invented in 1877, and Anaglypta were used for dados, while an enormous range of machine-made wallpapers flooded the market.

As in the eighteenth century, prosperous interior taste followed, in general, that of England. Elaborate curtain arrangements and pelmets, as proposed in Felix Lenoir's *Practical and Theoretical Treatise on Decorative Hangings or the Guide to Upholstery*, had been popular throughout the century. Festoon blinds were out and lavish curtains, often with swags and tail drapes and caught up in corded and tasselled tie-backs, extravagantly furnished new-fangled plate-glass windows. In more modest homes, chenille or velvet curtains, often with embroidered edging panels, were suspended from rings on curtain poles over windows and as *portières* over draughty doors. Venetian and roller blinds came in, the latter sometimes painted with decorative borders. Wooden board or parquet floorings were covered with rugs, bordered carpets of Wilton or Axminster weaves, or with red Turkey carpets, and a carpet-weaving industry in Persia catered for European demand. Hand-tufted rugs and rag rugs were created during long winter evenings by cottage industry, and fitted carpets began to be used at the end of the century.

The Victorians were collectors of objects from the past: early silver or Sheffield plate candlesticks and candelabra appeared on dining tables, sometimes combined with an elaborate centrepiece. *Garnitures*, combinations of candlesticks and ornaments, were popular mantelpiece decorations, sometimes with the addition of a clock in the centre and matching obelisks or vases, as at Cardy House. As with furniture, symmetrical groups and arrangements of ensembles were all-important and Victorian interiors were characteristically crowded with artfully arranged groups of pictures, drawings, prints and photographs, all carefully controlled. Victorian tourists surveyed picturesque landscapes through a frame held up to the eye and their houses were arranged as if the interiors, too, might be subject to visual analysis.

By 1890, the Forth Bridge, the greatest engineering achievement of Victorian Britain, straddled the estuary, its girders painted by the Edinburgh firm of Craig and Rose which also manufactured every kind of paint for every effect under the sun. Now a Victorian gentleman could travel comfortably from London to his Highland sporting estate and take back tales to perpetuate the myth of picturesque

'Scottishness' which the aristocracy, the monarchy and Sir Walter Scott had devised. Manufacturers leapt onto the bandwagon, putting tartan, stags and the Forth Bridge on everything from biscuit tins to furnishing fabrics, thus sugaring the harsh realities of Highland and working-class life in the nineteenth century. Robert Burns was urged out of the literary cupboard to be the voice of the ordinary Scot, the antidote to the 'menace' and, on the centenary of his birth in 1859, the *North Briton* periodical made a plea that the Bard should not be given up to the 'higher' classes. 'A man's a man for a' that' sang men who would not be seen dead wearing the kilt. 'Tartanry' to them was, as Michael Lynch suggests, substitute history. The Forth Bridge on the other hand, 'made in Scotland from girders', was a potent new symbol of excellence which extended to every industry from papermaking to Paisley shawl weaving.

Apart from the great new bridge, of all the products of the Victorian era, stained glass evinced the most distinct style. After the 1843 Disruption, the proliferation of churches offered new outlets for the decorative arts, including stained glass. The systematic post-Reformation destruction of medieval stained glass in Scotland left the studios free to create new designs, unhindered by historic prototypes and production-line copying which fettered Victorian stained glass production elsewhere in Britain. More than a hundred artists and literally hundreds of skilled craftsmen, working from around thirty documented studios, produced decorative glass for every type of building, including private mansions and villas, tenement closes, tearooms, libraries, cinemas, public baths and police stations. Studio owners tended to be well educated and they employed accomplished craftsmen with wide-ranging cultural interests and contacts whose methods of training laid the foundations of Scotland's excellence in what Michael Donnelly describes as this most democratic of art forms, whose popularity outstripped sculpture and murals. In Edinburgh, the studio of James Ballantine trained Frances Wilson Oliphant who collaborated with the genius of Gothic Revival, Augustus Welby Pugin and Stephen Adam, Scotland's leading designer of ecclesiastical stained glass from 1870. In Glasgow, John Cairney's studio trained Daniel Cottier, Charles Gow and John Lamb Lyon who pioneered stained glass production in Australia. Cottier, a pupil of William Morris, became Scotland's finest comprehensive interior decorator since Robert Adam. 'He became the catalyst and impresario for a highly gifted generation of artists at home and abroad,' says Donnelly; 'his activities as a connoisseur and picture dealer influenced public taste in painting in Scotland, Australia and America.'

Glasgow was an outstanding centre for stained glass production between 1870 and 1914 but by the 1970s, even in the Glasgow School of Art, its tremendous impact had been largely forgotten. Michael Donnelly, a former curator of Glasgow's People's Palace, began to research surviving records of the studios and to acquire panels for the museum. Sketch designs were recovered, domestic glass was rescued from derelict buildings or skips. Today the collection is the most comprehensive outside the Victoria and Albert Museum. 'However, fortunately for us all,' as Donnelly says, 'the best stained glass is still *in situ* in the hundreds of public and private buildings for which it was designed.'

Before the sun set, when Glasgow was still first city of the Empire, its stained glass, textiles, pottery, cast iron, marine and civil engineering products were exported to all parts of the globe. 'Made in Glasgow' became interchangeable with 'Made in Scotland' as a tag which consumers trusted as a guarantee of excellence, one in which the working classes took a quasi-masochistic pride which fell far short of making up for the hardships they endured in the slum interiors which most of them inhabited.

With the invention of photography interiors could be represented, without the translation of the artist's eye, albeit in sepia tint. However, the Victorians censored out subjects they regarded as unseemly or unworthy of documentation and, as happens in photography sessions for 'interiors' magazines today, rooms were carefully arranged beforehand. Ian Gow has made detailed studies of the photographs in the National Monuments Record of Scotland collection and comments on the photographs reproduced on the following pages. As he observes, 'while numerous photographers toiled before Mary, Queen of Scots' bed at Holyrood, almost nobody thought a kitchen worth the trouble unless it had belonged to Robert Burns, and the dictates of propriety banned photographers from the bedroom floor'.

In the early years there were practical problems to be solved in taking 'sun pictures' indoors, but after 1880 technological advancement ushered in the great age of interior photography. At one end of the scale there emerged magazines like *Country Life*, at the other private photograph albums bound in gilt and morocco recording well-to-do homes in large sepia prints. After it became practical to reproduce photographs in periodicals, articles about historic houses proliferated. 'All too often the photographer in his enthusiasm for the 'old' would temporarily edit the furniture the family actually used out of camera range in favour of a stiff line-up of Chippendale chairs,' observes Ian Gow. 'As one owner remarked after a visit from *Country Life*, the published result was 'worse than having burglars'.'

The lobby with standard Minton-tiled pavement and combined coat and umbrella stand. The walls appear to be stencilled with a bold pattern on a dark ground.

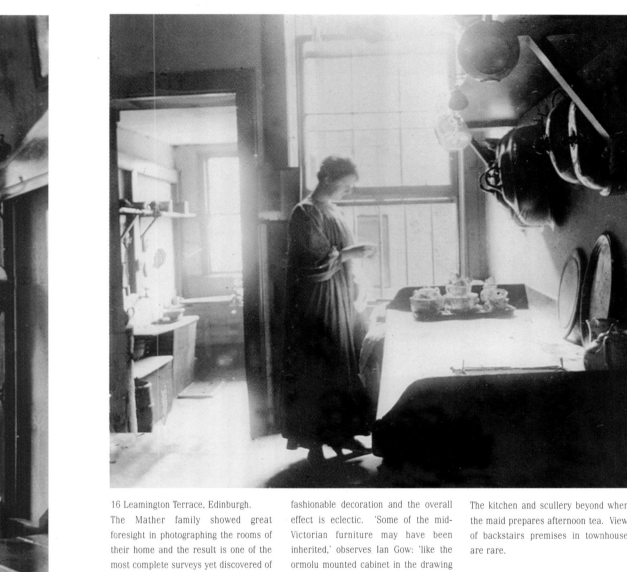

16 Leamington Terrace, Edinburgh.
The Mather family showed great foresight in photographing the rooms of their home and the result is one of the most complete surveys yet discovered of a late Victorian townhouse. Alexander Mather set up his married home in the 1880s within walking distance of his 'Millwrights, Engineers and Ironfounders' works in Fountainbridge. The Mathers brought up five daughters and a son in the house. Scrutiny of a photograph of the children performing as a sextet and of the photographs on the drawing room walls suggest music was a serious pursuit. The interior photographs, which were probably taken around 1905, reveal that the Mathers were not specially interested in

fashionable decoration and the overall effect is eclectic. 'Some of the mid-Victorian furniture may have been inherited,' observes Ian Gow: 'like the ormolu mounted cabinet in the drawing room and the parents' half-tester bed. The 'vaguely Queen Anne' diningroom furniture may have been purchased on the Mathers' marriage. Some of the more modish details and much of the bric-a-brac and flower arranging must reflect the input of the five daughters, but the Japonoiserie of paper umbrellas in the hearths and the shrine to Chinamania in the dining room were features of fashionable taste at the time the Mathers married.'

The kitchen and scullery beyond where the maid prepares afternoon tea. Views of backstairs premises in townhouses are rare.

Two corners of the drawing room where the wallpaper was probably printed in gold and the fashion for fitted carpets has passed. There are two aspidistras and the necessary *equipage* for afternoon tea on Mrs Mather's 'At Home' days.

The dining room with 'Queen Anne' suite, probably walnut, set on a conventional Turkey carpet. A high-dado paper adds a modish touch and the table is set for tea.

One of the children's bedrooms with family pet.

Laurencepark House, Stirling: this important photograph may record a decorative scheme by David Ramsay Hay, the pioneer interior decorator who was a protégé of Sir Walter Scott. The scheme was probably forty years old when it was photographed around 1880. Inspired by the rationalist spirit of the 18th-century Edinburgh Enlightenment, Hay was called 'the first intellectual house-painter' and after the publication of his first book in 1828, he began to apply scientific discoveries about colour theory to his trade. Hay hated wallpaper. In the damp climate paper became liable to 'putrefaction' and filled a room with 'the effluvia from the decayed animal and vegetable substances necessarily employed in this mode of decoration'. His solution was to oil-paint the walls and stencil them with geometric patterns in gold which, in grand houses, would quote from the family heraldry. A photograph on page 125 shows similar wall painting by the Edinburgh firm of Bonnar and Carfrae. The careful spacing of the motifs at Laurencepark House confirms that the walls are hand painted. Hay took seriously a room's aspect and function. 'This light and cheerful room is far from the standard pompous reception room of the time and may have been deliberately decorated as the sunny drawing room of a summer residence with plain painting of the plaster panelled ceiling which would more typically have been grained in imitation of oak. Wooden-slat Venetian blinds provided protection for the costly contents of drawing rooms like this one in which the curtains are chintz rather than conventional silk,' according to Ian Gow.

Round Drawing Room, 98 George Street, Edinburgh: a rare early comprehensive survey of a single room in a townhouse, taken in 1858, perhaps as a deliberate record of the family home of banker David Anderson of Moredun which was about to be purchased for Masonic Halls. Although the photographs are Victorian they offer an insight into the appearance of Edinburgh New Town houses in the 1820s when much of the furniture shown must have been supplied. An Old Master art collection, grand interior marbled columns and circular walls, distinguish the rooms which have been furnished *en suite* as was the custom, so that the connecting doors could be thrown open for larger parties or routs. The rooms have identical carpets and expensive flock wallpaper.

Oxenfoord Castle, Midlothian.

This photograph dates from the 1880s but little seems to have changed since 1840 when the 8th Earl of Stair commissioned the Edinburgh architect, William Burn, to enlarge and modernise Oxenfoord Castle. Burn was the leading country house architect of the day and his meticulous plans ensured that wealthy clients enjoyed luxurious and smooth-running houses finished with 'good and substantial work and nothing else is required', as one client was told. The drawing room and library (not shown) inter-connect to function as a single or larger unit as required and each is decorated with Elizabethan ceilings, matching carpets and crimson flock paper to show off the gilded picture frames.

However, as Ian Gow notes, there is a very unequal partnership in the drawing room's favour which retains the character of a state room of the Georgian period and has attracted the bulk of available funds for redecoration including additional ceiling ornaments and more gilding than the library. Although both chimneypieces are of statuary marble, only the drawing room boasts caryatids aspiring to sculpture. The drawing room is furnished with a suite in the costly 'Louis' revival style, a 'gorgeous' gilded overmantel glass, ormolu mounted antique French cabinet furniture, and cabinet pictures which rate as Fine Art. The library suite is plain and traditional Grecian style mahogany and leather, the art mere portraiture.

Drawing Room of an Unidentified Lady. Like the Oxenfoord Castle interiors, these views of the well-to-do drawing room of an individualist seem to have been taken around 1880 but decorated forty years earlier. Ian Gow comments that although the architect supplied something severely Grecian, the upholsterer has nodded to the fashionable 'Louis look' obligatory for drawing rooms of the period and introduced half-hearted rococo elements to his suite of chimney-glass, chiffonier, sofa and side-chairs. He observes a similar restraint in the standard floral fitted carpet which might have passed muster with mid-century design reformers who protested at the irrationality of trampling on bouquets of flowers. The pine woodwork has been transformed to imitate satinwood and there is a narrow gilt fillet round the plain oil-painted walls whose shade probably contrasts with the curtains, which would have been the starting point of the scheme. Crimson curtains against green walls was a favourite early Victorian scheme. Here a simple curtain replaces the elaborate dividing-doors of the Georgian period and the conservatory is separated by a window which keeps out damp more effectively than a door. The sewing machine and balls of wool suggests that the unidentified lady might have executed the Berlin woolwork on the chair.

7 Ann Street, Edinburgh.

Thomas Bonnar headed the firm of celebrated Edinburgh decorators, Bonnar and Carfrae, which his father founded. He wrote the biography of his uncle George Meikle Kemp, architect of the Scott Monument. Another uncle, the artist William Bonnar, was an early member of the Royal Scottish Academy and his father retired from the firm early to devote himself to easel painting. Many of these influences appear in this room. Bonnar read a paper to the Edinburgh Architectural Association, of which he was president, in 1879. In it he publicised his approach to decoration which favoured the romantically picturesque, and he admired the richly layered look of old family houses. At Ann Street he added vases and festoons to the plain Grecian cornice and replaced the press door with an elaborate glazed china-cabinet in Adamesque style. The wallpapers follow the fashion for dividing the wall with a high dado and the simple geometric pattern of the upper paper was probably selected to provide an unobtrusive background to the paintings and the suite of Aesthetic art-furniture, newly-made, perhaps to Bonnar's design. Despite a clutter of objects the room is restful with every item placed or hung to form part of a balanced arrangement.

Most of Scotland's thatched houses have succumbed to sheep and the elements but 12 Lower Ardelve has been saved, partly because when its last owner, Donald Mackenzie, was still alive both *Cairdean nan Taighean Tugha* (Friends of the Thatched Houses) and Historic Scotland had already taken an interest. The house is a listed building now under the protection of Historic Scotland. Shortly before he died Mr Mackenzie's house was thatched under the supervision of Jim Souness who is seen cutting reeds to dry out in bundles at the porch entrance.

Donald Mackenzie at his fireside in 1986. When the house was originally built, a single chimney would have sent peat smoke up through a central hole in the roof. Later, two fireplaces with wooden chimneys were constructed in each gable end of the house and burned wood rather than peat. Here, the Dutch oven which Donald Mackenzie's mother cooked in still hangs over the flames but he himself cooked on a Calor gas stove. Fortunately the interior of the croft house was photographed in 1986, otherwise a valuable record would have been lost forever. The contents of the house were removed after Mr Mackenzie's death and it is now an empty, though protected, wind and water-tight shell.

The parlour dresser overflows with treasured mementos, plates, cruets, jugs, egg-cups and the like and essential items of Donald Mackenzie's life: a Bible, alarm clock, torch, binoculars, bills and letters. Plates and jugs flow onto adjoining shelves where a Toby-jug shares space with special china including one or two Oriental items and a set of six cups and saucers commemorating the coronation of George VI. Donald Mackenzie remembered an itinerant tinker making a new metal jug handle to replace a broken china one. Cut paper shelf-edging with a rose pattern stands out from the poppy-motif wallpaper.

The bedroom where portraits of Donald Mackenzie's parents hang above the bed opposite a printed oil-cloth map of Scotland and the chest of drawers is a repository for prints, pictures, wash jug and basin, starched collars and a black homburg for Church attendance. A bedside table supports the Vicks Menthol Rub, a Gaelic Bible, Free Church magazines, other books in Gaelic and a volume of the writings of Descartes. Nineteenth-century patterned linoleum with a Chinese motif covers the floor. The characteristic Victorian fireplace is embellished with simple, strongly-coloured tiles and a brass hood. A romantic print of a scene from 'Young Lochinvar' hangs above (out of picture).

The exterior of Mount Stuart: 'a monument to pre-industrial values built from the proceeds of a industrial fortune', in this case the exportation of coal from Cardiff, was rebuilt by the 3rd Marquis of Bute, following a disastrous fire in 1877.

A view of the magnificently subfusc Great Hall of Mount Stuart, designed by Robert Rowand Anderson, which finds more than an echo in his entrance hall of the Scottish National Portrait Gallery, Edinburgh, built five years later. A star-studded vaulted ceiling with Zodiacal figures soars beyond vivid stained glass windows, three tiers of sandstone arcading embellished with stone and coloured marble columns and a palatial marble staircase. Not shown are three stained glass panels above the entrance bearing the arms of the three earldoms of Bute: Bute, Dumfries and Windsor. Much of the furniture in the house reflects honest craftsmanship. The 3rd Marquis came to share William Burges's disdain for Georgian veneers and Regency refinement.

A door off the Great Hall leads into the chapel built in gleaming white marble, tinged by the blood-red reflection of the lantern's stained glass. The design of the lantern was based on the Cathedral at Zaragoza, Spain.

The elaborately gilded domed Horoscope Ceiling in the main bedroom depicts the night sky on the day of the 3rd Marquis's birth and is surrounded by decorative painted panels of exotic African birds. This ceiling, and that of the Great Hall, reflect Bute's interest in psychic research and astrology which was influenced by Burges's neo-medieval perspective.

The second-floor conservatory under construction in 1986. Mount Stuart remained unfinished on the 3rd Marquis's death in 1900. Rowand Anderson complained that his client was 'never out of the mortar tub' and pleaded with him: 'Why not let it be finished, and off your mind?' Bute answered: 'But why should I hurry over what is my chief pleasure?' His dedication seems to have partly contributed to a continuity of interest in the architecture of their inheritance by his descendants including the late Lord Bute, the 6th Marquis, whose interests encompassed areas of the decorative arts including textile design and weaving and woodworking.

Between the marble arches and the leaded windows could be found the most up-to-date technology that the 1880s could provide. The house was supplied by a new waterworks built on the moors two miles above Mount Stuart, the very latest plumbing systems 'executed in the English style of workmanship' were installed, hot water pipes provided central heating throughout the building and electric light shone from hundreds of mosque lamps.

Set on a prominent site commanding views of fine rolling Border countryside, Ayton Castle was the archetypal dream house aspired to by the Victorian *nouveau-riche*, its towers and turreted gables signalling the wealth and authority of its owner. Ayton's architect James Gillespie Graham was unsurpassed in constructing dignified sandstone castles in the baronial style for aspiring clients. The building was finished in 1846 and a dining room extension was added by David Bryce in the 1860s. Gillespie Graham died before the interiors were complete, as did the first owner of Ayton, in melodramatic circumstances. Towards the end of the century there were plans to add a ballroom and other extensions, but the only other Bryce addition to the house was the alteration of the dining room window. From here, guests replete with wine and good food, might step out to admire from three sides the rich farmland of the Ayton estate and, on the horizon to the west, the perimeter of Hutton Castle, owned by the collector William Burrell.

Today the atmosphere of the library is very much as it was intended to be over a century ago – a pleasant sitting room for a gentleman. It has been restored according to the original intentions of GIllespie Graham and Mitchell-Innes. David Liddell-Grainger's ancestors who purchased Ayton from Mitchell-Innes's son in 1888 painted the room red. Now handsome and inviting, the warm orange brown walls are set off by an ornate light-olive and gold ceiling (not shown), also restored to the original colour. Leather bound volumes include *Letters of Queen Victoria*, Scott's *Poetical Works*, *Salmon Rivers of Scotland*, The *Berwickshire Naturalist* and a set of the *Waverly Novels*. The child's toys on the ottoman, the piles of magazines, family photographs, drinks tray and log basket indicate that, today, the room is enjoyed by everyone in the house.

Ayton's interiors display the peculiar mix of grandly formal and domestic rooms so beloved of Victorian country house owners. The hall is formal with informal corners and it comes as a surprise to see that there is no staircase. Grand staircases leading down to grand halls were generally favoured, not least by the ladies of the house and their guests who might sweep down, offering a preview of their finery to guests assembled below. But at Ayton the main staircase is hidden from view. It is a turnpike, or spiral stair, a re-interpreted classic feature of the Border keep and Renaissance

towerhouse. An internal stair, snug against the sharp winds that frequently buffet Ayton's hilltop, is a more comfortable route up to the corridors and bedroom even today. The walls of the elegant entrance hall and corridors were hand-painted in 1872 by the Edinburgh firm of Bonnar and Carfrae in a tracery of stylised flowers, including both the thistle and the rose. Today the stencilwork looks as good as new. The present owner has restored the rich ochre marbled pillars in the hall where visitors first arrive from the front door, as they did in medieval towerhouses.

But formality soon leads to the informality of a delightful corner where today a clutter of things lies out of place: country hats, riding hats, sunhats, family photographs, a table festooned with papers and books, a piano which someone is learning to play. The well-lit extension of the hall corridor offers a desk and chair in a quiet corner where house guests might write letters. Huge sheets of undivided plate glass were proudly installed in many country houses from the 1850s and these examples at Ayton, which echo the style of the hall's arches, are particularly elegant.

What was the master bedroom in Gillespie Graham's plan is the boudoir today. Elaborate plasterwork decoration is an unusual feature on doors, window frames and furniture rails. Festoon blinds in a traditional print emphasise the feminine character of today's room and glance back to the Georgian era. In contrast with the house's grand rooms, such as the dining room where elaborate curtains have recently been selected with guidance from the Victoria and Albert Museum, the boudoir is an informal room for evening relaxation.

Cardy House in Fife was built in 1871 for descendants of Alexander Selkirk, the famous castaway upon whom Daniel Defoe based the character of Robinson Crusoe. A Louis revival garden seat invites repose near a Muse, Atlas and an Arcadian youth only a little the worse for a century's weathering.

The scene might be a theatrical set for a murky Victorian drama: the hall and its landing are enriched with wall painting which occurs throughout the house: a decorative overlay of the original scheme, executed by James Darling of Edinburgh, a family friend. Red pine banisters, doors and panelling, an immense wooden chest, Victorian prints and a globed paraffin lamp on its original banister, Victorian china plantholders and pots, a musical box, remain as they have always been and a grandfather clock ticks away the decades on a corner of the stairs.

The dining room set for afternoon tea has changed little since David Gillies sat here with the Earl and Countess of Aberdeen and their guests after the statue of Alexander Selkirk was unveiled in the village in 1885. The mahogany table takes up much of the room with a button-back leather chair and a writing desk topped by a glass-fronted cabinet and sideboard embellished with a carved bird of prey. A glass case holds a century-old pair of silver-mounted bagpipes which belonged to a relative.

The highly polished black marble dining room chimneypiece and gilded overmantel. The splendid original 'garniture' consists of a heavy clock, a pair of Bohemian glass vases and a pair of theatrical bronzes and Indian elephants. The bell-pulls match the chimneypiece.

Detail of James Darling's later wall painting which suggests a strong interest in early painted decoration.

'Nothing but the best' was allowed into the drawing room dedicated to the arts where paintings hang in ornate frames, the work of artists who called at the house and left them as presents or in lieu of payment for some business transaction. Elaborate gilding survives in the ornamental ceiling, the frieze and massive curtain rails and picture rods finished with white porcelain and gilt

knobs match the door furniture and bell-pulls which still ring in the kitchen below although no servants wait there now to answer the call. A conventional Adam-revival marble chimneypiece supports one of a pair of overmantel mirrors which incorporate cameos of Queen Victoria as a young woman. Three generations of the Gillies family stare from daguerreotypes framed in red velvet and gilt. Violins

made by two musical brothers, William and Robert (who designed, built and raced their yachts *Quaver* and *Semiquaver* in the 1880s) stand in a corner near a small table inlaid with patterns for draughts and bezique. The tapestry curtains may belong to the second phase of redecoration of the house around 1890 which included James Darling's wall paintings.

Boxes collected by several generations include a Georgian knife-box, locked tea-caddy and 'apprentice boxes' made by members of the Gillies family.

Brass telescope in the bay window which commands spectacular views of the Firth of Forth and the opposite coastline of East Lothian. Holland blinds edged with lace and secondary lace curtains protect the contents of the drawing room from the full glare of the sun.

A corner of the drawing room dominated by an exotically veneered and gilded upright piano by Paterson and Sons of Edinburgh which supports a pair of ostrich eggs and other treasures. Grandly gilt-framed landscape paintings hang from chains and picture rods.

The Gothic headboard of the Scottish double bed and the white damask bedspread are woven with the motif: Cardy House, Largo, and the initials of its first householders DG and IG with the date 1889.

Bronze bust of Alexander Selkirk aka Robinson Crusoe by T. Stuart Burnett, commissioned by Cardy House's first owner, flanked by 18th century smugglers' liquor bottles which were found hidden under floorboards in a village house.

The rehanging of the glittering 18th-century chandelier, restored by the workshops of The National Trust for Scotland, symbolises Fyvie's most recent transformation. Fyvie Castle, with its important collection of portraits and other works of art, was purchased by The National Trust for Scotland in 1984, with the help of a generous grant from the National Heritage Memorial Fund. Several great families shaped Fyvie, one of Aberdeenshire's finest Renaissance strongholds, throughout six centuries: the Prestons, the Meldrums, the Setons, the Gordons and the Forbes-Leiths. With their architects, artists and craftsmen, all left their mark. A fortune amassed in the United States steel industry contributed to the castle's

Victorian flowering in the late 1880s when it was purchased by Sir Alexander Forbes-Leith, later Lord Leith of Fyvie, a descendant of the Leith Hays of Leith Hall and the Prestons of Fyvie. Lord Leith married Mary Louise January, an American heiress, and refurbished the house with all the opulence of the period. The castle's last tower was added in 1890.

Although the interiors had been redecorated between the wars, the house remained largely uninhabited for many years when the Trust took it over. Lord Leith had preferred to purchase new furniture and furnishings in London which reflected 17th and 18th century styles, rather than collect genuine period furniture to complement his

outstanding collection of portraits. The portraits, and a fine collection of arms and armour (Lord Leith's real interest) were restored in the Trust's workshops in consultation with the Armouries at the Tower of London. The Trust was able to set up the displays as Lord Leith intended, a circumstance which influenced its decision to emphasise the castle's late nineteenth-century interiors. The drawing room and the gallery beyond display a plush and electic taste, so admired by the Victorians. The outstanding collection of paintings includes a portrait of William Gordon by Pompeo Batoni, the Countess of Oxford by Sir Thomas Lawrence, and several works of Sir Henry Raeburn, Gainsborough, Opie and other masters.

Tartern and thistle-patterned chintz in Queen Victoria's sitting room at Balmoral Castle, 1857. Lithograph by Vincent Brooks.

Grand Victorian rooms invited lavish use of fabrics. Chintz, velvets and silks were favourites and inventions in the textile industry made their mass manufacture possible. Patterned chintz and tartan were introduced to Balmoral in 1855 as Lady Augusta Bruce noted in her diary. 'Chintz' derives from an Indian word that is now interchangeable with 'glazed cotton'. The fabric was originally manufactured in India for export to Europe where it has been popular since the seventeenth century in association with the relaxed elegance of the country house. Paisley pattern, another Victorian favourite, was inspired by Kashmiri floral motifs which by the end of the 18th century took the form of a stylised cone and, later, a formal scroll-like motif in an all-over pattern. These textiles became popular in the form of fine-woven 'Cashmere' shawls and are highly valued today. Edinburgh was a major centre of manufacture and the first to imitate Kashmir patterns in a brocade-weaving technique. The shawl industry in Paisley started as an offshoot of the Edinburgh industry and was the first to use the Jacquard loom in 1833. Paisley became the British centre of manufacture.

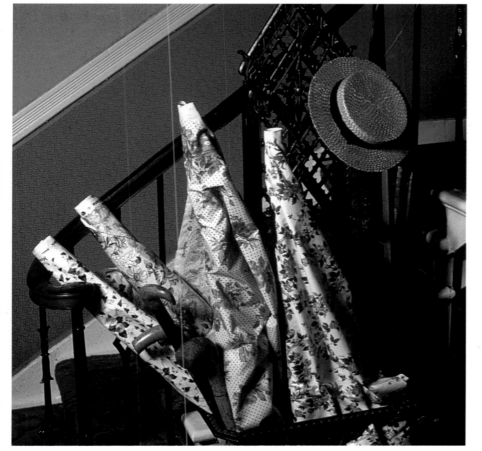

Trunks in the attic of Ardgowan House on Clydeside were discovered recently, full of Victorian furnishings. The fabrics had been carefully wrapped and marked with details of the rooms where they once hung. An inventory of 1843 evokes Ardgowan as 'typically' Victorian, cosy and cluttered. A British textile company, Ramm Son and Crocker, has reproduced the 'Ardgowan House Collection' shown here.

The smallest room of the 'Stevenson' house is really quite grand and retains more than an aura of yesteryear. Robert Louis Stevenson introduced his American bride, Fanny, to the family home in Edinburgh's Heriot Row in 1880. Through a window richly draped against chill draughts the Stevenson family overlooked a view which has scarcely altered since 'Leerie the lamplighter went posting up the street' as they attended to their *toilette* from porcelain accoutrements laid out on a tiled and marble washstand. James Pope Hennessy records that Fanny later confessed to her mother-in-law that she had struggled to lift the heavy ewer in her bedroom and assumed that: 'Heriot Row lacked wash-basins and running water because her parents-in-law could not afford such normal transatlantic comforts'. The truth was that, apart from grander country houses, British homes did not catch up with their American counterparts until the end of the 19th century but after the technological difficulties of piping large quantities of fresh water into city homes and draining out dirty water safely without polluting the drinking water supply had been mastered, plumbers' merchants offered a tantalising range of ways to keep clean. The 1892 catalogue of Wood and Cairns, an Edinburgh firm which is still in operation, promoted showers, shampoo taps, 'the spray' which played jets of hot or cold water into the bath from a raised hood above the bathtaps.

SUPERIOR
BRAMAH CLOSET
On Galvanised Iron Frame, Stuffing Box on Axle Bus
Rubber Seat Valve, Flushing Rim or Fan Basin
of the best Ware

Illustration from Wood and Cairns' 1892 catalogue.

The Victorian zinc bath 'built to cosset the human body' with original brass taps and fittings.

Fanny Stevenson might well have worn a silk dressing cape like this while attending to her *toilette*.

Contents of the cupboard including Sloan's Liniment, silver backed hairbrushes, shaving mugs and brushes.

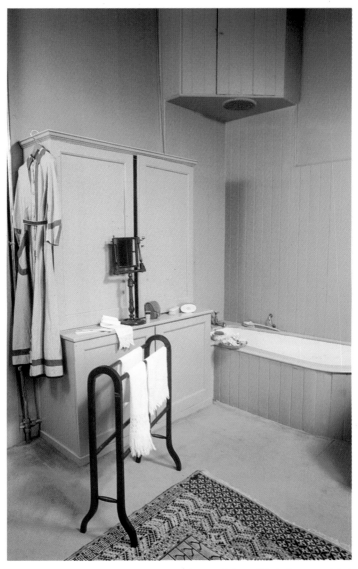

A general view of the bathroom, painted light blue in the belief that the colour repelled flies. A nanny's dress in rough cotton with horn buttons such as 'Crawfie' might have worn while her charge imbued inspiration for '*A Child's Garden of Verses*', hangs ready.

Stained glass had outstripped sculpture and murals as the most democratic of art forms by the 1890s. More than a hundred artists and literally hundreds of skilled craftsmen working from around thirty documented studios produced decorative glass for every type of building including churches, private mansions and villas, tenement closes, tearooms, libraries, cinemas, public baths and police stations.

'Gather ye Rosebuds while ye May', by George Walton, 1892. From a stair window in Glasgow, now in the People's Palace Collection.

'Music' by David Gauld for McCullough and Co., 1891. Private collection.

'Love and Audacity' by D. Cottier, 1873. People's Palace Collections.

'Water Sprite' by W. G. Morton, *c.* 1896.
People's Palace Collections.

The New Cafe Royal Hotel in Edinburgh which opened in 1863 is now the Cafe Royal which contains two legendary suites: the Oyster Bar and the Circle Bar. Both display rich Victorian interiors. 'An arcaded and mansarded *bombe surprise* which brought the French Second Empire to strait-laced Victorian Edinburgh' is how the late Colin McWilliam described it. The Oyster Bar was complete, much as it is today, by 1900 after the corner entrance and undulating pediment had been inserted. An earlier ceiling with gilded 'Jacobean' ribs, Irish harp and Scots thistle joins embossed gilded wallcovering, carved mahogany and mirrored screens, gilt light fittings, liver-coloured marble, black and white marble floor and fantastic stained glass panels and paintings: two Doulton pictures of a Cunard liner and a paddle boat painted by Esther Lewis. The stained glass windows by Ballantine and Gardiner represent six British sportsmen including a member of the Royal Company of Archers (the Queen's Bodyguard in Scotland) with longbow and a marksman with shotgun and stag. In 1900 in the Circle Bar (not shown) J. Macintyre Henry installed a massive mahogany chimneypiece and six Doulton tile pictures which had been shown at the South Kensington Exhibition of Inventions and Music in 1885. Six great discoveries are represented: three in printing by William Caxton's movable type, Benjamin Franklin's broadsheets, Robert Peel's patterns on calico; two in steam power by Watt and Stephenson; and one in photography by Niepce and Daguerre. The artists were J. Eyre, K. Sturgeon and W. Nunn.

EDWARDIAN SUMMER
1900 - 1910

'Art is the flower — Life is the green leaf'

The dining room at Ardkinglas House overlooks Loch Fyne. A Highland piper entertained the Noble family and their guests as they dined at long tables brought over from Ireland.

Britain embraced the twentieth century eager for change. Educated Scots recognised the need for illumination in public and international affairs, even as light lifted the atmosphere of their homes. Down came the heavy Victorian curtains, out went 'picturesque' clutter, antimacassars and the like, while white paint obliterated sombre colours and the revolutionary intervention of commercially generated electricity provided a clean source of light. Creative liberalism sought new outlets and would, Hugh MacDiarmid predicted: 'break through – Even in Edinburgh . . . in regeneration to a free and noble life'. John Buchan started a new magazine in 1907, the *Scottish Review*, 'to deal fully with all interests, literary, political and social with something Scottish in the point of view . . . such as Edinburgh had a hundred years ago'. Intellectuals looked back through the murk of Victorian pomp and religious hypocrisy, to a more vital age:

> *And 'civilisation' no longer like Edinburgh*
> *On a Sabbath morning.*
> *Stagnant and foul with the rigid peace*
> *Of an all-tolerating frigid soul!*

MacDiarmid, Buchan, Lewis Spence and others wanted to regenerate Scots as a living language. They vigorously attacked popular parodies of Scotland as a whimsical backdrop for tartan kilts, whisky, shortbread and porridge, which the likes of Harry Lauder continued to perpetuate, and they lambasted the false sentimentality of the Kailyarders who upheld what Trevor Royle has described as 'a never-never land of rural virtue, normally presided over by the discerning eye of the local minister'. Buchan, a son of the manse himself, was determined 'to eschew the politics and culture of the parish pump' as editor of the *Scottish Review*.

'The suckers of the wild Scots rose are beginning to show green underneath . . . You know our wild Scots rose? It is white, and small, and prickly, and possesses a sharp sweet scent which makes the heart ache,' said Hugh MacDiarmid, whose potent flower symbol became public a decade later. The suckers were rooted in the turn of the century when artists, craftsmen and architects began to clear out the lumber room of Victoriana. But they held on to the sophisticated taste of the few far-sighted collectors and artists of the Aesthetic Movement and the Arts and Crafts revival who, since the 1880s, had made the British house admired throughout Europe.

Edwardian Scots, like their European and American counterparts, felt a romantic desire to return to the intentions of an earlier age and closer involvement with the countryside. The American novelist Edith Wharton's book *The Decoration of Houses* (1898) was influential in promoting interior decoration as a branch of architecture, as the Adam brothers and their predecessors had advocated. 'Decorators know how much the simplicity and dignity of a good room are diminished by crowding it with useless trifles,' she wrote: 'It is surprising to note how the removal of an accumulation of knick-knacks will free the architectural lines and restore the furniture to its rightful relation with the walls'. Periodicals, particularly Edward Hudson's *Country Life*, had become potent carriers of the new taste and reacted against Victorian picturesque as fiercely as Mrs Wharton. But the magazine's ethos was more steeped than she in the archetypal dream of the British countryside: rolling lawns, apple trees, woodsmoke, country walks.

Country Life, founded in the late 1890s, was avidly read by 'old families' as well as romantic businessmen, including émigré Scots who dreamed of making a pile and retiring back to the old country to build a house or restore a ruin, although the magazine's coverage of Scottish houses was thin. The publication aimed to cover every aspect of country living as a response to the threat (and *fait accompli* despoliation) of industrialization and the growth of towns and cities. Declining industries had forced emigration and de-urbanisation by the turn of the century: Glasgow, Aberdeen and Dundee ceased to develop and Edinburgh maintained modest growth. After the war, English-style cottage or flatted villas replaced many old tenements and Scotland's transformation was typified by 'garden suburbs' at Hamiltonhill and Possil and, near Edinburgh, the exclusive semi-rural Colinton, Barnton and Corstorphine. Influenced by the Arts and Crafts revival, Edwardian free style with a Scottish touch might display crowsteps, stair towers or diminutive caphouses but the authoritative finials and towers of the baronial style relaxed into much simpler constructions harking back to the Renaissance or, over the border, to England's Tudor Revival. Barnton residents, notes John Gifford could go between the golf course and English half-timbered and red tiled homes and hardly notice the difference, while Art Nouveau influences, too upstart for Edinburgh, infiltrated Glasgow.

In 1900, Charles Rennie Mackintosh (1868–1928) spent his honeymoon on the Holy Island of Lindisfarne, some sixty miles south of the Scottish border, returning in 1901, the year which marked a transition in his creative life and resulted in the poetic expression contained in a manuscript of the period which has more than an echo of

MacDiarmid's rose symbol: 'Art is the flower – Life is the green leaf. Let every artist strive to make his flower a beautiful living thing – something that will convince the world that there may be – there are – things more precious – more beautiful - more lasting than life.'

The art historian, Roger Billcliffe, has observed that Mackintosh's marriage to Margaret MacDonald was probably the catalyst which inspired the evolution of the flower drawings into pictures in their own right and not simply sketches as ideas in his pattern-book of decorative details. Nature, and wildflowers in particular, inspired Mackintosh's furniture and the decorative details of his architecture. Petals, seed-pods, flower stems and tendrils were all part of the design vocabulary he had amassed as pencil sketches ever since his student days. But under the timeless tranquillity of Lindisfarne's influence, he began to produce exquisite, mature watercolours inspired by individual flowers: *Sea Pink, Bugloss, Pimpernel, Yellow Clover, Purple Mallows, Milk Thistle, Mustard-seed Flower, Storksbill, Cranesbill, Brook Weed* and *Hound's Tongue*.

By extraordinary coincidence, Charles Rennie Mackintosh and Edwin Lutyens, England's and Scotland's most outstanding Edwardian architects, both drew inspiration from Lindisfarne in the first year of the century. In this charmed, leisured period, when summers were remembered as long and sunny, and the privileged took proper August holidays (which frequently included adventurous excursions in leather-upholstered motor cars equipped with picnic hampers), Edward Hudson arrived in Lindisfarne accompanied by Peter Anderson Graham, editor of *Country Life* and author of *Highways and Byways in Northumbria*. They were scouting for suitable properties to include in the magazine and, although it would be some time before Lindisfarne Castle achieved that distinction, Hudson was immediately impressed by its potential. Finding the place unoccupied, the two warmed to adventure and, scaling crags and walls, laid siege to its interior. It was to sight Scots invaders and to stop them from scaling its walls that the castle was originally built. In reality, the castle was more of a fort and, according to a seventeenth-century report, 'a daintie little fort' at that. The castle's last inhabitants before Hudson's 'siege' had been coastguards who left behind the disorder and squalor associated with a place which has lost its true function. Far from putting Hudson off, the fort's dereliction encouraged him to believe that he might be able to make something quite remarkable of it.

Enchanted by the island and struck by the potential of the fort on the crag as a holiday home, with stunning seaviews, bound round with an Arthur Ransome-like sense of adventure, by January 1902 Hudson had negotiated its purchase from the Crown. His excitement must have been further inflamed by the contemporary passion among the literary circle he moved in for restoring and inhabiting ruined castles, which were not always easy to come by. He summoned his friend, the architect Edwin Lutyens to the site with a telegram: 'Have Got Lindisfarne'.

Seen from the mainland or from the sea, Lindisfarne Castle's romantic profile on Beblowe Crag hints at a place as legendary as any Arthurian knight or Edwardian architect might have wished for. Like St Michael's Mount in Cornwall and Mont-Saint-Michel in Normandy, Lindisfarne Castle functions as a visual lure which magnetizes people and draws them off the road of humdrum, everyday lives. Closer inspection, though, reveals a different reality: the building on the rock is small for a castle; its roofs are finished with dark-orange pantiles. It is, in fact, the Edwardian villa Lutyens created for Hudson in a bower of valerian atop the basalt crag where fulmars nest. Lutyens built upon the 'daintie little forte', endowed it with Tudor Revival features (portcullis, buttresses, mullion windows, beamed ceilings, hammernail doors) and topped it all off with a pantile roof.

Lutyens admired Mackintosh and made a point of taking tea at the Willow Tea Rooms in Sauchiehall Street when he was in Glasgow. Almost the same age as Charles Rennie Mackintosh and Edward Hudson, at thirty-three Edwin Lutyens was already the leading country house architect of his day. His reputation was built on his 'Surrey picturesque' period, but recent work had revealed him to be eclectic and original with an unusual sympathy for texture and the use of local materials. His work at Lindisfarne did not disappoint. Lutyens created a series of strong, sparse interiors retaining exposed stone walls married here and there with whitewash. The atmosphere of the interior derives from an intriguing blend of medieval and Dutch features, the latter particularly appropriate given the location of the castle on old east coast trading routes with the Low Countries. And the unpretentious, solid wooden furniture set on herringbone brick floors covered with old patterned carpets and decked with shining brassware and pottery, suggests a place to which travellers have returned from inspiring adventures. Lutyens built only one Scottish house, Greywalls, Gullane, and brought Gertrude Jekyll with him to create the garden as she had at Lindisfarne. A contemporary of Lutyens and Mackintosh, the architect Robert Lorimer (1864–1929) added a kitchen and dining room in 1910.

New families and romantic businessmen wishing to restore or build in the new style in England aspired to have Lutyens as their architect. In Scotland they wanted Robert Lorimer who became known as the 'Scottish Lutyens'. As Mark Girouard observes, both had the gift of all good architects, of sensing what their clients wanted and giving it to them in heightened and transmuted form. Lorimer met Herman Muthesius, the German cultural attaché in London, who subsequently wrote *The English House* and was the first critic to recognise Lorimer's outstanding contribution: '[he] saw the virtues of the unostentatious old Scottish buildings with their true hearted simplicity, and plain almost rugged moderation . . . Today Lorimer's achievements in house building are the most interesting to compare to those of the Mackintosh group . . . Scotland will attain also a national perfection by his efforts.'

Charles Rennie Mackintosh's gift was extraordinary, so transcendently rooted in a Scottish vocabulary yet with such innovative panache that few clients dared commission him and even the four or five who did, like William Blackie, were not prepared to give him a completely free hand. The Blackie family wished to supplement the furniture Mackintosh made for Hill House with their own, thus compromising his interior design by the addition of objects, books and personal paraphernalia. When The National Trust for Scotland accepted the house in 1982, with a substantial grant from the National Heritage Memorial Fund towards the restoration of the structure and the interiors of the house, several of the major pieces Mackintosh designed for the house were missing from the drawing room and Mr Blackie's dressing room. The dining room was furnished with the Blackie's own Victorian furniture but the Trust has begun to replace odds and ends of reproduction Mackintosh furniture in the room with pieces more in keeping with the Blackie's taste.

The debate continues about the difficulties the Trust faces in determining a housekeeping policy for Hill House. Roger Billcliffe's view of the matter would probably be endorsed by the many visitors who flock there: 'Are Mackintosh and the Blackies to be treated as equal partners in the restoration of the house, even if that means the imposition of the Blackies' taste in decoration and furnishing on top of that of Mackintosh? The house was acquired for the nation because of the importance of its design and the international reputation of its designer, not because of its connections with the Blackie family . . . Is the display of a spinning wheel in the first floor ingle, for instance, justified by the insight it gives us of the Blackie family, despite its total incongruity in a house which marks the entry of Scottish architecture into the 20th century?'

Most of the furnishings from 78 Southpark Avenue, where Mackintosh and Margaret MacDonald took up residence in 1906, were presented to Glasgow University in 1945. Prior to the demolition of the house in 1963, a survey was carried out and all salvageable fitments were removed and incorporated into the reconstruction of the interiors within the Hunterian Art Gallery. The original decorative intentions of Mackintosh have been respected and the collection displays the purest and most complete of his Glasgow Style interiors. The contents of the Mackintosh Wing demonstrate his career as a furniture designer from 1896 to 1906 and include items which attracted attention at the exhibitions in Vienna, Turin and Moscow in the early years of the century. Mackintosh was carried shoulder-high through the streets of Vienna after one of the exhibitions and European artists and craftsmen arrived in Glasgow in significant numbers to see the work of the Glasgow School for themselves.

Roger Billcliffe has documented the evolution of Mackintosh's unique style in *Charles Rennie Mackintosh: The Complete Furniture, Furniture Drawings and Interior Designs* and recent research has revealed the artistic personalities of other designers discussed in *The Glasgow Style 1880–1920* while the more commercial designs of Wylie and Lochead, Glasgow's leading house furnishers have been studied by Juliet Kinchin in the *Journal of the Decorative Art Society*. Glasgow Style furniture, much of it made by colleagues of Mackintosh, is on permanent display at Kelvingrove Art Gallery and Museums and the Fine Art Society has created a room in the Mackintosh style, with original pieces, within its Glasgow gallery. Here, the doors were made by Keppie and Henderson, the architectural firm which supervised the restoration of the Willow Tea Rooms in Sauchiehall Street. A fireplace designed by George Walton is incorporated with furniture by George Logan and John Ednie who worked for Wylie and Lochead, producing furniture in the Mackintosh style.

Edinburgh's equivalent of the Willow Tea Rooms was Crawford's Tea Rooms in Princes Street, designed by Robert Burns. Like Mackintosh, Burns was a pupil of Glasgow School of Art and although both artists developed an Art Nouveau style, each gave it unique expression. Burns was known as one of a circle of artists associated with Patrick Geddes, the pioneering biologist and town planner, which also included Phoebe Traquair and John Duncan. It was under Burns' direction that Whytock and Reid made the furniture and the sculptors Phyllis Bone and Pilkington Jackson made the hanging signs and carved finials of the staircase of the Art Nouveau interior. Robert Burns' exotic panel *Diana and her Nymphs*, recently acquired by the National Galleries of Scotland, is a last remaining treasure from the venture.

Glasgow Style was as original as Edinburgh Style was restrained, but both made an impact on British Edwardian taste. 'Edinburgh Style' has been less researched than its Glasgow counterpart, presided over by Mackintosh, the undisputed genius of the age. Edinburgh's leading protagonist was Robert Lorimer who, like the Glasgow designers, had a School of Art for a seedbed. The Edinburgh School of Applied Art had been founded by Rowand Anderson in 1892 and imbued with his obsession that students should master the details of every important historical style. He stressed nationalistic 'Scottishness' for its own sake. Lorimer's furniture was idiosyncratic, as Peter Savage's biography conveys, but some of the most refined furniture of the Edinburgh School could pass for elegant antiques, so deeply were the craftsmen of Edinburgh cabinet making firms like Whytock and Reid and Morrison and Co. imbued with the spirit of the past.

W. R. Reid, director of Morrison and Co., furnished his home, Lauriston Castle, with fine examples of Edinburgh Style and the careers of other contemporaries are documented by Elizabeth Cumming in *Arts and Crafts in Edinburgh*. As Ian Gow comments: 'The Edinburgh designers displayed such mastery that in items like Scott Morton and Co.'s reproductions of 'Adam' chimneypieces, the best of the new surpasses the old, much to the confusion of present day architectural historians. For example, the difficulty in deciding how much, if any, of eighteenth century Manderston is still visible is a tribute to Rowand Anderson's pupils who went on to staff the Edinburgh firms.'

The sole survivor of these firms is Whytock and Reid of Edinburgh, whose approach still reflects Rowand Anderson's ideals and who eagerly buy back every past product of the firm as it comes onto the market, since they are particularly well placed to recognise the merits of its craftsmanship, fastidious choice of timbers and fluent design. They also hold the finest decorative art archive in Scotland and preserve the working drawings for the furnishings of any of the Edwardian palaces which they supplied. A particularly evocative group of drawings, picked out by Ian Gow, is labelled 'Dinner Gongs', some of which were made to take their client's 'Own Tusks' and other trophies of big game hunting.

No doubt Sir James Miller brought back many trophies from the South Africa War in 1901. He immediately selected the Edinburgh architect John Kinross to come up with a scholarly but eclectic late eighteenth-century style for Manderston. Manderston had to be a palace filled with superior interiors which would satisfy his 'old family' wife, the Honourable Eveline Curzon, sister of George Nathaniel Curzon soon to be Viceroy of India, who had been brought up in the sumptuous Kedleston Hall. John Kinross's links with Rowand Anderson and the 3rd Marquis of Bute, for whom he restored Falkland Palace, had earned him a reputation as a skilled designer of impeccable taste. And Kinross found in Sir James the perfect client, who on being asked how much the remodelling of Manderston should cost, replied, 'It doesn't really matter'.

Curzon, renowned for his fastidious and scholarly taste as much as for his chilly pride, had to be impressed, as John Gifford has observed. And 'this most superior person', who placed high value on intellect and breeding, could have found little other than wealth to commend his new brother-in-law. For Sir James's father, William, had been born in Leith and made a fortune of several million pounds as a merchant in St Petersburg before becoming a Liberal MP and purchasing Manderston (then a substantial 1790s house set in parkland) in 1864. It was Sir William who had supplied a new front in what John Gifford calls 'the French Renaissance Rothschild style favoured by the *nouveaux riches* of the day . . . and it must have looked both old-fashioned and rather too crudely ostentatious for a bride brought up in the neo-classical grandeur of Kedleston Hall'.

John Kinross drew inspiration for the huge Ionic portico of his entrance façade and west addition from the garden front of the eighteenth-century house whose interiors he now extended and remodelled. The ceilings were modelled on Robert Adam's designs for Kedleston and other quotations from Adam's work, including Syon's Doric screens, and the opulent silvered balustrade based on the design for the staircase in the Petit Trianon at Versailles. And the interiors allowed the circulation of guests as a palace might: married guests approached the hall down the silvered stair and met the bachelors there beside the vast chimneypiece on an inlaid marble floor which echoed the design of the ceiling. Under the central dome they might watch the approach of neighbours invited to dinner through the portico where their outer vestments were carried by maids to the marble-walled cloakroom. Then guests approached the dining room through the ante-room, glowing with back-lit peach-coloured alabaster panels and a stucco relief of Diana, a romantic allusion to Sir James's love of the hunt. After Sir James Miller restored Manderston it was a palace, though not conventionally so. A ball was held in 1905 to mark the completion of one of Edwardian Scotland's most superior interiors but its owner, Sir James Miller, who commissioned its extension and improvement, was dead of a cold three months later.

If Manderston was a throw-back to Victorian proconsular pretensions, Ardkinglas exemplified the current taste for country houses that, to quote Vita Sackville-West, were 'essentially part of the country, not only in the country but part of it, a natural growth'. In 1904, the Scots-Canadian wife, and Lily, the eldest daughter of Sir Andrew Noble, were yearning for the beauty and romance of Scotland's west coast and succeeded in tempting the family patriarch away from the good shooting of north-east England where they spent their summers. In 1900 Sir Andrew Noble had become chairman of Lord Armstrong of Cragside's Tyneside armaments empire, which six years later commissioned *Dreadnought*, the prototype of the series of warships which would soon symbolise British maritime might. That same year, work began on the construction of Ardkinglas, Noble's new country house on the shores of Loch Fyne. For the Edinburgh architect, Robert Lorimer, designing a country house for such a wealthy client was the fulfilment of a dream and Ardkinglas was to become his favourite project. There, he and his craftsmen enjoyed artistic freedom and they created an exterior which reduced the neo-baronial proportions and rejected the towers favoured by clients of the likes of Gillespie Graham or David Bryce in favour of symmetry, order and sympathy with the landscape.

In the matter of the house's interiors, Lorimer accepted Lily Noble's desire, inspired by her reading of Henry James's *Spoils of Poynton*, that at Ardkinglas there should be 'not an inch of painted paper from one end of the great house to the other'. Walls were panelled or plastered, simply-carved dressed stone complemented handsome parquet floors, lightly-grained wooden doors and shutters were carved with an echo of medieval linen-fold. Lorimer's house exudes cordiality, well-being and an understanding of the Noble family, whose daughters breathed a freshness into its spaces while their father rumbled to his end even as the distant Armstrong-made guns augured the close of the Edwardian era.

It lives on, though, within the interiors of a house in a leafy West End Glasgow terrace which have changed little since the first decade of the century. There must be many others, but few are as accessible as this one, whose owner allowed the cameras in. Everyone who has lived in this particular house has treasured its effects and hesitated to throw anything out. Much has faded or worn, some items have had to be replaced or renewed, but everything has been respected: the Japanese metallic watered silk wallpaper and colour scheme in the drawing room, the leather-look wall covering in the halls and the dining room, the original light fittings in their Art-Nouveau variations, the Art Deco cupola and fully equipped billiards room. In the present owner's lifetime the carpet linoleum will never be replaced, the now collectable Edwardian twisted stem candles will never be lit, nor will the Beeston boiler in the kitchen, the mangles and wringers in the laundry, be removed. The elegant Edwardian silver tea service on its mirror-like 'Edward's' tray and the silver cruet sets will continue to be brought out for special occasions, though, and family friends will be offered a ducking in the Shanks bath and shower, designed for the Great Glasgow Exhibition of 1911.

The terrace was built between 1902 and 1910 for what we now call 'middle managers': the manager of North British Locomotives lived here alongside the manager of a steel foundry, lawyers and the like, while the great Glasgow merchants lived in Park Circus and the doctors in Royal Crescent. But here were more modest family homes, substantial and uncompromisingly handsome in their square dressed-stone exteriors with modest balconies, terrazzo steps leading to pedimented entrances, grey-slated roofs with, here and there, a no-nonsense turret. The development was designed by John Archibald Campbell and put up by one of the many speculative builders of the time. The builder, Mr Smellie, went bankrupt before the scheme was complete and his downfall is recorded, even today, in the craggy protuberance of corbels and quoins destined never to join up with the next number in the terrace.

The prospectus attracted buyers with its stipulation that the terraces were to be for domestic purposes only. There would be 'no tenements' in the scheme and 'no stables'. None of the first owners were sufficiently well off to afford a horse and carriage though a few must have aspired to drive a motor car. However, the area was well supplied by the tramcar system and a suburban railway which gave speedy access to the centre of Glasgow, so that the men of these houses could, and usually did, return for lunch. A cook general and a house parlourmaid lived in, their quarters lit by gas in contrast to the rest of the house which boasted the new fangled electricity. Daily help was brought in when needed for rough work like cleaning out fires and carrying coals and washing kitchen and pantry floors.

For the Edwardians, home was where the hearth was, and the development plans for the terrace stipulated several fireplaces and chimneys to each house. Coal fires were used in winter and the new radiant heaters in summer. And in smaller-scale emulation of the grander suburban houses springing up on the edges of towns and cities, the villas were built with well-equipped kitchens, pantries, laundry and boiler rooms and maids' quarters. So much was built into its appointed place that the present owners find a lack of cupboard space for the 'new technology' that is required to maintain homes of this size today in the absence of maids.

Edwardian Glasgow offered a plentiful supply of cheap servant labour but in other parts of Britain this was thrown into jeopardy by competing jobs in offices and factories which offered better hours and remuneration and more independence. Still, even in Glasgow, 'better' servants had to be tempted by houses that were easy to clean and manage and their live-in quarters improved dramatically. Commercial laundries, urban and suburban grocery and vegetable stores with vans to collect and deliver, vacuum cleaners, baths and washbasins, electric light and more efficient kitchen ranges offered the middle classes a standard of living previously undreamed of.

In this West End house where the Edwardian grandfather clock ticks on, the 1980s floor washer and polisher is both a boon and a 'glorious toy' in the words of the present owner. But pleasure in its use is indulged in only twice a year as 'a bit of dust' is preferable to wearing out the now irreplaceable linoleum and parquet flooring. Not that this house is a museum. Far from it. Its resident came here, to her grandparents' house, as a child of five in the 1930s with her two brothers and her parents who were returning to Scotland from an assignment in Burma and Ceylon. The house had been purchased from its first owner in 1925 and, since the march of progress was slow in those days when things were made to last, hardly anything had altered since 1910. The first owners were obviously in touch with cultural Glasgow, though, and opted to replace the standard round overmantel mirror in the drawing room with a rose painted roundel by Stewart Park of the Glasgow School.

The returning grandchildren shared the day nursery and the night nursery and the little girl grew up and never left the house, so that her memories have the veracity which most people lose as they travel, from house to house, away from their roots. Every part of the house, as well as its objects, is imbued with a rich patina of recollection which she relates with relish to anyone interested who happens to 'stumble across me and is interested in the Edwardian period'. Thus the fortunate visitor is invited to appreciate the past, not through the eyes of a museum curator or interior designer, but through a living link with someone who recalls that 'when Grandfather returned to work after lunch, Gran retired to the drawing room for a rest on a sofa bought from Gardners of Glasgow: I'm sure she embroidered the cushions to match the dusky pink walls.'

Afternoon tea was brought up later by the maid and placed on the table. The morning room was 'Gran's' base for the first part of the day, which was devoted to organising the house and meals, instructing the servants, receiving tradesmen or her dressmaker. No doubt, as was the custom, she herself would make trips into town, to the best stores and supplier, to hand select tea, dessert fruits, furnishings and the like. Furnishings from 'Gran's' era fill the house today with an overlay of her offspring's possessions. Among these are sturdy pieces in the Glasgow Style purchased from the most respected Glasgow firms of the day, notably Gardners (taken over by Martin and Frost) and Wylie and Lochead (absorbed into the House of Fraser). Toffolo Jackson executed the terrazzo steps, which decayed and had to be replaced, but the terrazzo entrance hall remains. American Globe Vernika bookcases exported to Glasgow at the time found their way into thousands of middle-class homes, as did sets of engravings like the ones in the hall and the Templeton carpets which cover many Glasgow floors today. Here we are both in the present and the past and all around is a lively demonstration of what it was to be Edwardian. Life was more relaxed than in Victoria's reign, a fact reflected in these furnishings and objects whose form and design is lighter, more graceful and altogether more friendly.

But, ironically enough, the last word on the Edwardian house was communicated by a German, Hermann Muthesius, who was sent to Britain at the expense of his government to study contemporary design. *Das englische Haus* (1904) caused a sensation when it was published in Germany, and if two wars had not intervened, perhaps the book would have appeared in English translation before 1979. 'Who but a German could appreciate the important part played by the window cleaner in British domestic architecture?' asks Ian Gow, whose anthropological insights into the trivialities of domestic life enliven his own book about Scottish interiors. 'Muthesius is amazed by the beauty of the average English dinner table, daily decked with exotic flowers (freely and cheaply available in response to mass demand) in marked contrast to rough checked tablecloths of the German Inn. Elsewhere in his book he becomes lyrical in appreciation of the merits of British plumbing, recalling the celebrated and contemporary essay on the same subject by the Austrian Adolf Loos.'

The domestic aspirations of Edwardian Scots were, by and large, similar to those of the rest of Britain and it is ironic that a German writer reflected them more vividly than anyone else had done. *The English House* is a moving tribute to a domestic ideal soon to be shattered by the Great War. Lily Noble's cordial summers in the fresh spaces of Ardkinglas, and the summers of countless other Edwardians, would never be the same again, as the distant sound of Armstrong-made guns augured the era's end.

Robert Lorimer's design for furnishing the drawing room at Balmanno Castle, Perthshire *c*.1916: as Ian Gow observes, 'clients who had not yet formed their own antique collection or who did not trust their own powers of picturesque arrangement, could bring in Lorimer's team to supply the effect almost off-the-peg. Although this drawing is among Lorimer's office papers in the National Monuments Record, it originated from Whytock and Reid, then, as now, the Edinburgh's premier firm of cabinet makers and upholsterers. The use of detailed room plans like this was common in France and Whytock and Reid had Parisian contacts. The style of the drawing, however, is home-grown and reflects habits instilled by Rowand Anderson at his revolutionary Edinburgh School of Applied Art, which opened its doors in 1892.' The 16th century towerhouse, Balmanno Castle, was renovated by Lorimer for W. S. Miller, a Glasgow shipping magnate.

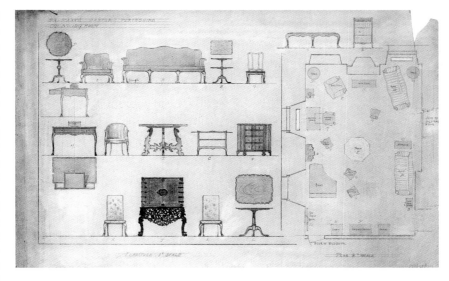

F. T. Tennant's Drawing Room at Hyndford, North Berwick, painted by Patrick G. Adam: Patrick Adam was renowned for his ability to capture the spirit of interiors, and since few Lorimer colour schemes survive in their entirety, this painting has particular value. Lorimer crated an almost identical room in his own house at 54 Melville Street, Edinburgh, and wrote movingly of the pleasure it gave him. Here, comments Ian Gow, the simple bareness reflects a forceful rejection of Victorian clutter. 'The antique collection has an air of *The Spoils of Poynton*, but the arrangement can be seen as merely a watered-down version of the picturesque aesthetic taste of the 1880s, when collecting first became a craze. The cult of the white drawing room, too, is in aesthetic taste and the panelling is notably French rather than Scots in inspiration.'

The Longcroft, Helensburgh, *c.* 1908: By the turn of the century, most of the large numbers of photographs of Edwardian rooms which exist are the work of professional photographers. Though technically imperfect, these informal snapshots are of particular interest. The family consists of A. N. Paterson, a successful Glasgow architect, his wife Maggie Hamilton, who was a well known embroiderer, and their two children. Alexander Paterson studied at the École des Beaux Arts in Paris, a training which, as Ian Gow says, gives his work a certain urbanity. He displayed his possessions carefully against the restrained background of his new rooms at The Longcroft. The drawing room, filled with flowers, for which Guthrie and Wells made a panel depicting the *Muse of Embroidery*, is 'almost a bower dedicated to Maggie Hamilton's art.' Both The Longcroft and Mackintosh's Hill House nearby drew inspiration from the baronial style which found dramatically different expression in the hands of the two architects.

Bedroom in a Kirkcaldy Villa designed by William Williamson *c.* 1910: 'The fitted bedroom was an Edwardian hallmark which arose from an obsession with hygiene. Fitted cupboards could not harbour dust, immaculate white painted panelling was designed to show every mark, and simple curtains could be readily and frequently washed.' Ian Gow's observations apply to a bedroom in an unidentified Kirkcaldy Villa which he adds, seems almost a parody. 'Williamson, the architect could not budge his client from the complex coziness of the four-poster bed in favour of a more avant-garde brass or painted iron bedstead prophylactic against dust and dreaded vermin. The bare floorboards, however, show slight willingness on the owner's part to put cleanliness before personal comfort. However, this bedroom betrays deep-seated provincialism and compromise that Edinburgh luminaries like Lorimer would have found irritating to work against.' Williamson designed the Burgh Buildings in Kirkcaldy.

The Pleasance, Gullane, photographed by Bedford Lemere, *c.* 1904: The architect Sydney Mitchell's own interiors reveals an Edwardian obsession for accurate historical styles re-enacted in different rooms of a house. The living hall was included by Hermann Muthesius in the illustrations to his revolutionary book *Das englische Haus* (1904). Ian Gow describes the room as 'mixing its metaphors with cottage style and an Art Nouveau frieze; yet it is an agreeable and remarkably chaste essay in the Queen Anne style.' It is a light and comfortable room which would look fashionable today.

The Hill House, Helensburgh: William Blackie, one of the most successful publishers of his day, operated the business from Glasgow with branches throughout the Empire and employed, as his art director, Talwin Morris, the distinguished artist in the Glasgow Style who designed the Art Nouveau covers for Blackie's books and recommended Charles Rennie Mackintosh for the Hill House commission. Mackintosh specified stone dressings around the entrance elevation whose abstract arrangement of shapes, solid and void indicates its importance.

Charles Rennie Mackintosh photographed by Craig Annan around 1894.

A Mackintosh chair in reflected sunlight in the Glasgow School of Art Board Room. The American novelist Edith Wharton's book *The Decoration of Houses* (1898) was influential in promoting Edwardian interior decoration as a branch of architecture as the Adam brothers and their predecessors had advocated: 'Decorators know how much the simplicity and dignity of a good room are diminished by crowding it with useless trifles,' she wrote: 'It is surprising to note how the removal of an accumulation of knick-knacks will free the architectural lines and restore the furniture to its rightful relation with the walls'.

Entrance hall: Mackintosh did not have an entirely free hand in furnishing the house and in addition to several major pieces he designed specificlly for the house, some key pieces from the drawing room and Mr Blackie's dressing room have disappeared. The Blackie family modified Mackintosh's interior design with redecoration and furniture, china and other personal paraphernalia. One of Mackintosh's most elegant clocks (not shown) is carefully integrated into the design of the hall, the most complicated space in the house, which displays Mackintosh's assurance. With the exception of one chair and the carpet the hall is much as William Blackie knew it. The original hall carpet is in the collection of the Glasgow School of Art.

Drawing room: Mackintosh provided the Blackie family with an elaborate window seat beyond which the garden and the distant Firth of Clyde could be seen. The National Trust for Scotland recently restored the drawing room and the carpet and the RIAS has replaced the wall stencils but the unsympathetic black ceiling remains to be replaced with the warmer 'plum' tone designated by Mackintosh.

In William Blackie's day his bedroom was not this stark white cube. The walls were decorated with an overall pattern of briar roses to a height of about 4'6" and two embroidered panels by Margaret and Frances MacDonald. The chair in the corner is a 1950s reproduction which masks the now-blocked-off door to Mr Blackie's dressing room.

Corner of bedroom: the chair was designed by Mackintosh some months after the fitted furniture had been installed in the bedroom. Its purpose was purely decorative and its position within the plan of the room quite specific in relation to the organic shapes and colours: whites, pinks and greens, of the wardrobe and the wall stencils.

Manderston: the restrained style of the garden front of the 18th century house which Edinburgh architect, John Kinross, was engaged to remodel by its owner, Sir James Miller, inspired this new entrance facade and great Ionic portico. Bachelor guests entered the house by the west wing under a relief of Diana, the goddess of the chase, set over the door leading to the gunroom, a marble-floored octagonal entrance hall where foxes' masks, bears and stucco fans are displayed. In this masculine domain a mahogany door opens into a lavishly appointed washroom with marble basins designed to cope with the mud of a day's sport.

Hall: Manderston's opulent interiors display 'proconsular pretensions' rather than reflecting the Edwardian preference for interiors which sympathised with the surrounding countryside. The chimneypiece and stuccoed overmantel of the main hall as well as other architectural and decorative features at Manderston were copied from Robert Adam's designs for Kedleston Hall, Derbyshire, where Lady Miller was brought up and where Sir James proposed to her.

Peach-coloured alabaster panels, glowing from light behind, guide the way to the dining room with its deep, richly decorated wall recess containing on the sideboard a display of urns and candelabras in blue John, a semi-precious stone mined in Derbyshire. The 'Chippendale' dining chairs are fine Edwardian reproductions like most of the furniture at Manderston. Later in the smoking room, male guests could summon a footman to bring a drink by way of one of the telephones installed by Sir James.

Although the design of the main staircase is closely modelled on that of the Petit Trianon at Versailles the silver plated balustrade and solid brass hand rail are unique. It leads up to eighteen family and guest bedrooms.

Ballroom: Curtains woven with gold and silver thread lend the ballroom an opulent richness which is matched by the furniture. Architectural features display a sumptuous mixture of Robert Adam and Louis XVI influences. The dining room ceiling at Kedleston Hall was the model for the ceiling whose primrose ground and white mouldings echo Sir James Miller's racing colours and pick up the embossed velvet of the walls.

The bathroom boasts a silver-plated bath set in a marble-clad recess.

Neo-baronial Ardkinglas on the shores of Loch Fyne was Robert Lorimer's favourite project. Built as a country home for the Noble family, with a hydro-electric power house and dam, new farmyard, cottage and kennels, it is now a permanent residence at the centre of a thriving local seafood industry. Lorimer's sectional drawings indicate harling which was never incorporated, leaving the local green granite to glitter under Scottish slates from Easdale.

Portrait of Robert Lorimer, by his brother John, at work as an apprentice to an Edinburgh architectural practice whose partners included Rowand Anderson.

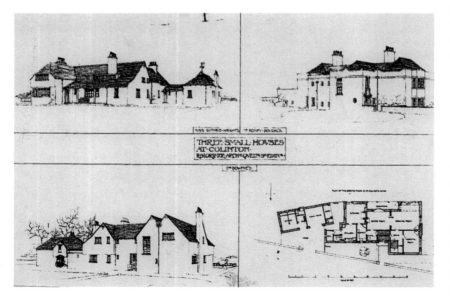

Rowand Anderson built some fine Victorian villas in Colinton and lived there himself. Later, in 1893, Robert Lorimer built a new harled cottage-style house for Miss Guthrie Wright, the first of several 'cottages' he built in the area which started a fashion for small houses inspired by both Scots and English tradition.

The chimneypiece in Ardkinglas's opulent saloon was carved from a solid five ton block of granite and the ceiling is decorated with Roger Fry's painting which 'nobody much cared for but had not the strength to get rid of'. Ardkinglas was well endowed with fireplaces which were continually lit to keep the house dry since the roof was never insulated.

Lorimer designed the curvaceous door furniture in the Saloon which is typical of the style throughout the house.

The hall, lit from both sides, overlooks the loggia with views down the loch as far as Inveraray. An array of the most advanced meteorological equipment prepared visiting Edwardian sportsmen for the worst West Highland weather as they set off for a day on the hills.

The large kitchen staff of Edwardian Ardkinglas is a thing of the past but the handsome tile-lined kitchen is still fully used.

Most of the bedrooms at Ardkinglas share magnificent lochside views and each has its own character, some with bays and some without, and decorated ceilings: flat, segmental or coombed. The Cartington Room (not shown) has a built-in bed in the best Highland tradition and a stylish Lorimer corner fireplace, while the Anastasia Room ceiling is decorated with Lorimer's vine design modelled by Sam Wilson of Edinburgh in the plasterwork style that delighted the young Dorothy Noble.

Lord Armstrong's home at Cragside, Northumberland, was among the first to be lit by electricity and a hint of rivalry is evident between the first chairman of Armstrong and his successor, Andrew Noble. Ardkinglas boasted not only a hydro-electric plant of its own but also an internal telephone system.

An up-to-the-minute shower sends jets from all directions. There was no local supply of electricity so Lorimer harnessed the water power of the adjoining burn and a dam above the burn fed the generator house.

This tranquil terrace in the West End of Glasgow, near the Great Western Road, was built between 1902 and 1910 for what we now call 'middle managers'. The manager of North British Locomotives and of a steel foundry lived here with lawyers and the like.

A simplified Georgian-style balustrade marks the boundary of the upper landing, below a cupola of Art Deco stained glass where the family circulated from the dining room, morning room and service rooms below to the upstairs drawing room, four bedrooms and bathroom. Furnishing here is minimal: 'Grandfather's' collection of Victorian etchings and prints hang on the leather-look walls and one of the house's American Globe Vernika bookcases stands out of the picture.

The present owner has had the original brown kitchen paint stripped back to pine. Otherwise the kitchen is much as it always was: stone sink set low 'for tiny West Highland and Irish maids', central scrubbed table, built-in glass fronted shelves and cupboards, tiles, pulleys and linoleum. The architect provided only one socket – for ironing – unable to imagine the many electrical gadgets which would flood the market as the century progressed. In this house where the grandfather clocks tick on, the 1980s floor washer and polisher is both a 'boon and a glorious toy' whose use is indulged only twice a year since 'a bit of dust is preferable to wearing out the precious linoleum or parquet flooring'.

A handsome Beeston boiler set within a tiled recess next to a cupboard full of kitchen utensils. The two contemporary ceramic cats were purchased at the People's Palace.

The dining room decorated in greens, browns and neutral shades, exemplifies the restrained good taste of a prospering middle-class Edwardian family. Although much of the furniture was added later, some pieces purchased from the Glasgow firm of Wylie and Lochead remain with the original leather-look wall covering and suspended chimneypiece with Art Nouveau decoration (not shown). The table is set for dinner with silver, china, glass and candlesticks which belonged to 'Gran' and the present owner's mother.

The lady of the house received morning calls in this ground floor room overlooking the front door. Chairs brought back by the family from the Far East and appropriate Sanderson wallpaper have been added. Otherwise the room with its Edwardian light fittings, parquet flooring, chimneypiece and fireplace tiles has hardly changed at all.

Part of an Edwardian silver tea set on a tray of beaten metalwork typical of the work of the Glasgow School.

Miscellaneous glass and crockery was kept in the Morning Room cupboard with its decorative glass panels, ready to equip informal meals which were sometimes taken here. Morning Rooms had disappeared as separate women's rooms in grand houses but lingered in middle-class Scottish homes as tranquil places which caught the morning sun.

Everything in the drawing room reflects middle-class Glasgow taste, from the Bechstein upright piano near the window (out of picture) to the Glasgow Style display cabinet. The furniture is placed much as it was at the turn of the century: a semi-circle of upholstered chairs and sofa with the fireplace as the focal point and occasional chairs and cabinets against the walls. The three-piece suite was purchased from A. Gardner and Sons, Ltd. of Glasgow in 1905 and the original worn tapestry was recovered in uncut moquette in 1960. A Mackintosh-style chair from Gillow of Lancashire stands beside the fine Glasgow Style display case inlaid with Art Nouveau-inspired decoration which holds family memorabilia. The window is shaded with a half-blind to protect the room's contents from bright light. The lamp 'ready to glow pinkly' with its original bulbs is a period piece, seldom lit now, above the Edwardian card table. Most of the houses in the street were supplied with round mirrors set into the drawing room overmantels, but the owners of this particular house chose instead a painting of roses by Glasgow Boy artist, Stewart Park. The room was warmed by a coal fire in winter and a radiator in summer. The ceiling was redecorated thirty years ago but the original plasterwork swags on the frieze still echo the 'true lovers' knots' round the central light fitting. The Templeton carpet has been lifted to display the parquet flooring but the fireside rug is original. Although the watered silk wall covering has faded over the years, all in all, the room looks much as it did when 'Gran' took afternoon tea here.

The main bedroom contains a handsome suite of Glasgow Style furniture purchased from Gardners of Glasgow: 'His and Her's' wardrobe, bed, washstand and dressing table display characteristic metalwork, cut-out 'flying birds' and 'heart' motifs and inlaid panels. Embossed wallpaper and tiles are part of the original 1910 redecoration of the house. The Shanks bath and shower were purchased from a selection on show at the Glasgow Exhibition of 1911.

Interior view of The Dovecot's main studio where today's weavers still work on traditional high looms

Dovecot Studios: original spools and contemporary wools.

Exterior of The Dovecot Studios, now the Edinburgh Tapestry Company, which was commissioned by the 4th Marquis of Bute to produce tapestries for his properties. William Morris (1834–1896), imbued with the ideas of John Ruskin, pioneered his discovery that in manual work and craft it was possible to regenerate a whole style of life. He founded the firm of Morris, Marshall, Faulkner and Company in 1861 and gathered round him artists including Burne-Jones, Rossetti, Ford Madox Brown and Philip Webb. The company moved to Merton Abbey in 1877 where tapestry work was inspired by those of the Middle Ages and the Dovecot enterprise sprang directly from this root. The early works were created under two master weavers from Merton.

Diana and her Nymphs, Robert Burns (1869 – 1941). National Galleries of Scotland. Edinburgh's Willow Tea Rooms equivalent was Crawford's Tea Rooms in Princes Street designed by Robert Burns who was one of a circle of artists associated with Patrick Geddes, the pioneering biologist and town planner, which also included Phoebe Traquair and John Duncan. It was under Burns' direction that Whytock and Reid made the furniture and the sculptors Phyllis Bone and Pilkington Jackson made the hanging signs and carved finials of the staircase of the Art Nouveau interior. Robert Burns' exotic panel *Diana and her Nymphs*, is a last remaining treasure from the venture.

The Prince of the Gael, the great unfinished Bute tapestry, originally commissioned to partner *The Lord of the Hunt*, which hangs in the hall of Mount Stuart, has remained on its loom at the end of the Dovecot Studio ever since its weaving was interrupted by the Second World War. The tapestry's heavy hatching was influenced by the Arts and Crafts Movement's desire to recreate medieval methods.

The Hall, Kinloch Castle, Rhum.
(Leeming and Leeming, *c.* 1899 – 1903)

BIBLIOGRAPHY

Apted, M. *Painted Ceilings of Scotland.* (HMSO, 1966)

Bamford, Francis. *A Dictionary of Edinburgh Furniture Makers, 1660-1840.* (The Furniture History Society, 1983)

Billcliffe, Roger. *Mackintosh Watercolours.* (London, John Murray, 1978)

Breeze, David J. (ed.) *Scottish Castles and Fortifications.* (HMSO, 1986)

The Buildings of Scotland: *Edinburgh.* Gifford, McWilliam, Walker and Wilson. (Penguin Books, 1984)

The Buildings of Scotland: *Fife.* John Gifford. (Penguin Books, 1988)

The Buildings of Scotland: *Glasgow.* Williamson, Riches and Higgs. (Penguin Books, 1990)

The Buildings of Scotland: *Highlands and Islands.* John Gifford. (Penguin Books, 1992)

The Buildings of Scotland: *Lothian.* Colin McWilliam. (Penguin Books, 1978)

Chambers, William. *A History of Peeblesshire.* (Edinburgh, Chambers, 1864)

Chinnery, Victor. *Oak Furniture: The British Tradition.* (Antique Collectors Club, 1979)

Defoe, Daniel. *A Tour Through the Whole Island of Great Britain.* (Penguin Classics, 1986)

Donnelly, Michael. *Glasgow Stained Glass: A Preliminary Study.* (Glasgow Museums and Art Galleries, 1981)

Fletcher, Bannister. *A History of Architecture.* (New York, Scribners, 1967)

Girouard, Mark. *Life in the English Country House.* (New Haven/London, Yale U.P., 1978)

Gow, Ian. *The Scottish Interior.* (Edinburgh University Press, 1992)

Hartley, Christopher. *House of Dun.* (National Trust for Scotland, 1992)

Lynch, Michael. *Scotland: A New History.* (Century, 1991)

Mackay, S. *Lindisfarne Landscapes.* (St Andrew Press, 1995)

Mackay, S. (ed.) *Scottish Victorian Interiors.* (Edinburgh, Moubray House Press, 1986)

Mackay, S. (ed.) *Scottish Edwardian Interiors.* (Edinburgh, Moubray House Press, 1987)

Mackay, S. (ed.) *Scottish Georgian Interiors.* (Edinburgh, Moubray House Press, 1987)

Mackay, S. (ed.) *Scottish Renaissance Interiors.* (Edinburgh, Moubray House Press, 1987)

Master Weavers: *Tapestries from the Dovecot Studios: 1912-1980.* Scottish Arts Council exhibition catalogue. (Canongate, Edinburgh, 1980)

Muthesius, Hermann. *The English House.* (London, Crosby Lockwood Staples, 1979)

New Town Conservation Committee. *The Care and Conservation of Georgian Houses.* (Oxford, Butterworth Architecture, 1986)

Pennant, Thomas. *A Tour of Scotland in 1756.* (Perth, Melven Press, 1979)

Royal Commission on the Ancient and Historical Monuments of Scotland. *Peeblesshire, Volume II.* (HMSO, 1967)

Royle, Trevor. *Precipitous City: The Story of Literary Edinburgh.* (Edinburgh, Mainstream, 1980)

Sanderson, Margaret H.B. *Robert Adam and Scotland.* (SRO and HMSO, 1992)

Savage, Peter D. *Lorimer and the Edinburgh Craft Designers.* (Edinburgh, Paul Harris, 1980)

Thomson, Duncan. *The Life and Art of George Jamesone.* (Oxford, Clarendon Press, 1974)

Thomson, Duncan. *Painting in Scotland 1570-1650.* (Trustees of the National Galleries of Scotland, 1975)

Treasures of Fyvie. (HMSO, 1985)

INDEX